John Paul II

Pastoral Visit to St. Louis

John Paul II

Pastoral Visit to St. Louis

on the Occasion of the release of *Ecclesia in America*
"The Church in America"
by His Holiness Pope John Paul II

Dedicated to His Holiness Pope John Paul II
Pastor of the Universal Church

Foreword by
Archbishop Justin Rigali

ISBN 0-9675728-0-0

Printed in the United States of America

Cover Photo:
Nancy Wiechec,
Catholic News Service

Title Page Photo:
Cathedral Basilica
of Saint Louis,
John Wm Nagel

Back Cover Photo:
The Jubilee Doors,
Cathedral Basilica
of Saint Louis,
Tim Umphrey

Front Cover Quote:
Pope John Paul II,
*As The Third Millennium
Draws Near,* 16

Table of Contents

Foreword   2

Acknowledgements   3

The Pastoral Visit   4
    Pope John Paul II (Karol Wojtyła)
    Planning the Pastoral Visit
    This Pope, the Papacy
    The Synod for America
    The Pastoral Visit to St. Louis,
       January 26–27, 1999

Introduction   30
    The Paths to Conversion,
       Communion and Solidarity

Chapter One   32
    The Path of Conversion

Chapter Two   66
    The Path to Communion

Chapter Three   100
    The Path to Solidarity

Transcripts of the Words of His Holiness
    Pope John Paul II in St. Louis   134

Foreword

by Archbishop Justin Rigali

As the seventh Archbishop of St. Louis, I have been blessed to witness the glorious response of so many people to the Pastoral Visit of His Holiness Pope John Paul II to St. Louis. The historic visit of the Holy Father will be, for many in St. Louis, a once in a lifetime event—an occasion of vital importance to the Church of St. Louis and the entire St. Louis community.

I am very pleased to present this commemorative volume which chronicles some of the memorable images of the Pastoral Visit and all of the talks given here by His Holiness on January 26–27, 1999.

The Holy Father came to our Gateway community so "that the power of salvation may be shared by all" (*As The Third Millennium Draws Near,* 16). He led and joined the Catholic community in prayer and empowered us to follow Christ by taking his message to the world. He also came to encourage the community of St. Louis to commit to a greater understanding and cooperation in confronting the demands and challenges of a new century.

Pope John Paul II reminded us that we have so much to be grateful for as we approach the end of this second Millennium. He urged a renewal of spirit and a sense of solidarity among peoples as we look forward to the new century. As the Holy Father stated in his homily at the Evening Prayer Service: "…*the eve of a new Millennium*—by any standard a decisive turning-point for the world. As we look at the century we are leaving behind, we see that the human pride and the power of sin have made it difficult for many people to speak their mother-tongue. In order to be able to sing God's praises we must relearn the language of humility and trust, the language of moral integrity and of sincere commitment to all that is truly good in the sight of the Lord."

No event since the 1904 World's Fair has placed St. Louis so forthrightly on the forefront of the international scene. And St. Louis was prepared to embrace an event of this magnitude. I want to offer the expression of deep appreciation to those individuals who planned the Papal Visit, to those who offered generous support, to the thousands of unselfish and committed volunteers, and to all who came together with the Holy Father to pray and to listen to his words. All of these individuals ensured the success and splendor of this Pastoral Visit.

Let us pray that the love and enthusiasm instilled in us by the Holy Father will continue to thrive for years to come. We will always look back on his final words to us in St. Louis with sentiments of thanksgiving and elation:

"I will always remember St. Louis.

I will remember all of you.

God bless St. Louis!

God bless America!"

Acknowledgements

Vicars General

Most Reverend
Edward K. Braxton, V.G. **(A)**
Auxiliary Bishop of St. Louis

Most Reverend
Joseph F. Naumann, V.G. **(B)**
Auxiliary Bishop of St. Louis

Most Reverend
Michael J. Sheridan, V.G. **(C)**
Auxiliary Bishop of St. Louis

Reverend Monsignor
Richard F. Stika, V.G. **(D)**
*Chancellor/Coordinator
of the Papal Visit*

Core Planning Committee

Reverend Monsignor Richard F. Stika, V.G.
Chancellor/Coordinator of the Papal Visit

Reverend Monsignor Ted L. Wojcicki
Vicar for Planning and Evangelization

Reverend Monsignor Dennis Delaney
Director of Communications

Reverend Henry J. Breier
*Secretary and Master of Ceremonies
to the Archbishop*

Ms. Jennifer Stanard
Vice Chancellor for Special Projects

Mr. John M. Britt
United States Secret Service

Papal Visit 1999 Honorary Co-Chairs

Mr. August A. Busch III **(E)**

Senator John Danforth **(F)**

Mr. Stan Musial **(G)**

Ms. Blanche Touhill, Ph.D. **(H)**

Executive Committee

Reverend Mr. Robert Brooks

Mrs. Hazel Harrison

Ms. Marie Jeffries

Mr. Jerry Ritter

Mr. Anthony Sansone, Sr.

Dr. Virginia Weldon, M.D.

Venue Chairs

Reverend Robert Finn
Airport Arrival & Departure

Reverend Paul Niemann
Evening Prayer

Reverend K. Robert Smoot
Youth Gathering

Reverend James Swift, C.M.
Papal Mass

Reverend Monsignor James Telthorst
Pre-Event Papal Mass

Committee Chairs

Mr. Patrick Barron
Ticketing and Invitations

Deacon Frank Chauvin
Accounting/Finance

Reverend Monsignor Dennis Delaney
Communications Committee

Sister Cathy Doherty, SSND
Decor

Mrs. Rainey Fahey
Disability Access

Mr. David Farrell
Fund Raising

Mr. & Mrs. William Guyol
Hospitality

Reverend Vincent Heier
Ecumenical Greeting

Mr. Patrick Henning
Printed Materials

Mr. George Henry
Catholic Education Office

Reverend Monsignor
Robert Jovanovic
Hotels

Mr. Alfred H. Kerth III
Civic Issues

Ms. Virginia Klein
Volunteers

Mr. Mark Lamping
Papal Commemoratives

Colonel Robert Lowery
Safety/Security

Deacon Joseph Marcinkiewicz, Jr.
Motorcade

Mr. Edward Martin, Jr.
Social Awareness Issues

Mr. Joseph McGlynn, Jr.
Motorcade

Reverend Thomas Molini
Hospitality

Mrs. Juli Niemann
Accounting/Finance

Sister Mary Roch Rocklage, RSM
Ticketing and Invitations

Dr. John Romeri
Music

Mr. Zip Rzeppa
Community Issues

Mr. Joseph Shaughnessy
Transportation

Mr. Wayman Smith III
Civic Issues

Reverend Monsignor John Unger
Follow up

The Pastoral Visit

Pope John Paul II (Karol Wojtyła)

Pope John Paul I died in his sleep on the evening of September 28, 1978, after a pontificate of only 33 days. The world was stunned. There had hardly been an opportunity to know him, but already he had touched many with his wry smile. As the College of Cardinals gathered two weeks later to elect his successor, it was widely assumed that they would pay closer attention to the question of the new Pope's health and strength. On October 16, 1978, after a conclave of only two days, Cardinal Pericle Felici, the Cardinal Protodeacon, appeared at the window of St. Peter's Basilica to announce to the world the magnum gaudium, the great joy, that the new Pope was Cardinal Karol Wojtyła and that he would reign under the name of John Paul II. A Pole, the first non-Italian pope in 456 years, Papa Wojtyła was 58, robust, and unexpectedly mediagenic. The world was instantly captivated.

Pope John Paul II set the theme for his papacy in the homily of his Inauguration Mass on October 22, 1978, in St. Peter's Square: "Be not afraid," he said—the words of Jesus to his apostle Peter. Some years in later, in the best-selling book, *Crossing the Threshold of Hope,* the Pope asked: "Of what should we not be afraid? We should not fear the truth about ourselves." Indeed he has never wavered in the proclamation of that truth, and tireless evangelizer that he is, he firmly locates that truth in the proclamation of Jesus Christ as the truth itself.

(Above) The young
Fr. Karol Wojtyła

Karol Wojtyła was born on May 18, 1920, in Wadowice, a small town in southern Poland. He was to know hardship from an early age. He lost his mother when he was only 9 years old, his brother just three years later. In 1938, with his father, he moved to Cracow, where he enrolled in the historic Jagiellonian University to study Polish literature. In these early years he showed an interest in acting and entertaining, in chess-playing, in soccer, in writing poetry, and in singing and playing the guitar. But student interests were quickly eclipsed by the German invasion of Poland in 1939. Most of the Jagiellonian faculty were immediately imprisoned and killed by the Nazis, and Wojtyła himself was forced to take employment in a limestone quarry. In 1941, his father died. In 1944, Karol himself was nearly killed when hit by

a Nazi truck. Remarkably enough, in these dark days of his life, he also wrote plays and poetry, performed in an underground theater company, and acquired an interest in the writings of the mystics.

His years in the world of work had a lasting effect on his life and his priesthood. Here are his own words:

> *I knew quite well the meaning of physical labor. Everyday I had been with people who did heavy work. I came to know their living situations, their families, their interests, their human worth, and their dignity. I personally experienced many kindnesses from them. I made friends with the workers. Sometimes they invited me to their homes. Later, as a priest and Bishop, I baptized their children and grandchildren, blessed their marriages, and officiated at many of their funerals. I was also able to observe their deep but quiet religiosity and their great wisdom about life.*

This is perhaps one reason why so many people today feel touched by the ministry of Pope John Paul II. He understands and acknowledges ordinary faith lived out in the simple life.

In 1942 he began studies for the priesthood at a clandestine seminary, working at the same time in a caustic chemical plant. He and another young Pole, Jerzy Zachuta, would often serve Mass in the Archbishop's private chapel. One day Jerzy did not come for Mass. He had been taken during the night by the Gestapo and his name appeared on the list of Poles who were to be shot. Such was the routine terror of those years.

In that same small chapel, on the Solemnity of All Saints, November 1, 1946, a year after the liberation of Poland and the end of World War II, Karol Wojtyła was ordained to the priesthood. As a young priest he was assigned to study theology at the Pontifical Angelicum College (now the Pontifical University of St. Thomas Aquinas) in Rome, writing on the mystic, St. John of the Cross. He completed his studies and successfully defended his dissertation in 1948, although he could not afford to publish it; the doctorate was actually granted by the Jagiellonian University upon his return to Poland. In his first months back in his homeland, he threw himself into pastoral work, concentrating his attention especially on young people. He was an outdoor enthusiast, and memories abound of the young priest, and later the bishop, hiking, skiing, and canoeing—usually in the company of many others. It was a pattern that was to continue even after he was assigned to further studies. His young friends called him then and still call him *"Wujek,"* or "Uncle."

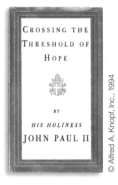

In 1951, at his bishop's insistence, he pursued sabbatical studies, again at the Jagiellonian University, this time in philosophy and ethics. He began teaching first at the Jagiellonian and then at the Catholic University of Lublin, where he was appointed Professor of Ethics. With his book, *The Acting Person* (1969), he established a name for himself in contemporary philosophy, and was eventually known even to philosophers outside his homeland.

In 1958 at age 38 he was named Auxiliary Bishop of Cracow, and was at the time one of the youngest bishops in the world. It was in this capacity that he attended the Second Vatican Council in Rome, where he played an active role, especially in the formulation of the documents, *Dignitatis Humane,* the Declaration on Religious Liberty, and *Gaudium et Spes,* the Pastoral Constitution on the Church in the Modern World. He was named Archbishop of Cracow in 1963, and became a cardinal in 1967. He was then 47 years old.

In 1960, he published his most famous book, *Love and Responsibility,* in which he combined an explanation of traditional Catholic values on family and sexuality with an acute pastoral sense of the circumstances in which those values are lived. He is said to have been consulted extensively by Pope Paul VI in the writing of *Humanae Vitae,* the controversial encyclical that restated the Catholic rejection of contraception. He was also invited by Pope Paul VI to preach the 1976 Lenten sermon series to the members of the papal household.

The Poland in which he ministered had seen its liberation from wartime German occupation turn into postwar Communist subjection, as the Iron Curtain so famously described by Winston Churchill descended across Eastern Europe in the late 1940s. Since Polish nationalism had always been linked to its roots in Latin Catholicism, unique among the Slavic nations, Poland again turned to its religious faith to deal with the new occupation. The strength of that faith made Poland a place apart in the Communist Warsaw Pact community. The Roman Catholic Church in Poland was too strong to be dealt with summarily, and the leadership of the Church was able to extract concessions from the Communist government that allowed considerably greater religious expression there than elsewhere in the Communist world. Wojtyła continued in that tradition, dealing at the same time with the complications of the Vatican's *Ostpolitik,* the effort to deal with Communist governments in a more conciliatory fashion. It is said that he had some disagreements at least in emphasis with Cardinal Stefan Wyszynski, the Archbishop of Warsaw and Primate of Poland, but these he never made public. As newly-elected Pope, he refused to allow Wyszynski to kneel in obeisance before him, and in one famously photographed scene from shortly after his election, the two men knelt to each other in an embrace, each in tears.

The list of milestones in his papacy is remarkable: a revision of the *Code of Canon Law* (1983); the promulgation of the *Catechism of the Catholic Church* (1990); the publication of 13 encyclical letters, including the statements of moral doctrine, *Veritatis Splendor,* The Splendor of Truth (1993), and *Evangelium Vitae,* The Gospel of Life (1995). He survived an assassination attempt in 1981, tumor surgery in 1992, and a broken femur in 1994. At Christmas of 1981, he met with his would-be assassin, to offer forgiveness. He wrote an international best-selling book, *Crossing the Threshold of Hope,* in 1994.

He is widely credited with a key role in the collapse of European Communism in the early 1990's. With the apostolic letter, *Tertio Millennio Adveniente,* As The Third Millennium Draws Near (1994), he inaugurated an extensive period of preparation in the Church for the Great Jubilee of the year 2000, the beginning of the third millennium of Christianity, and has often expressed a fervent hope that he may lead the Church across that historic threshold.

Perhaps the most conspicuous feature of his pontificate are his travels. As Bishop of Rome, he immediately set about the task of visiting all the parishes of his new diocese. As Supreme Pontiff, he has embarked on an even more vigorous program, 84 visits to 119 countries, more than 700,000 miles traveled. His visit to Mexico City and to St. Louis was his 85th journey, to be followed in June by a lengthy trip to his native Poland. In all of these travels, the pattern is nearly the same: crowded motorcade routes, massively attended liturgies and events, awe-struck witnesses from the poorest to the most powerful, ecumenical and interfaith encounters, a special outreach to youth, and always, at the center, the uncompromising proclamation of Jesus and the Gospel.

In October 1999, Pope John Paul II observed the twenty-first anniversary of his election to the See of Peter, now one of the longest pontificates in history. Many in the Church have already begun to apply to him the accolade of greatness. His biography is a remarkable one, and even more remarkably a providential preparation for the office he exercises with such consummate skill. He is fluent in eight languages. He is a world-class teacher and pastor, at once a towering intellectual and a man of the people. But above all, by the universal testimony of those who know him and work with him, he is a man of prayer—deep, heartfelt, and lengthy prayer, surely the source of his personal energy. The Church has truly been blessed by his ministry.

Planning the Pastoral Visit

Papal Visit 1999

The historic visit of His Holiness Pope John Paul II to St. Louis is graphically depicted in a logo. The principal element of the emblem is the image of Christ crucified which is a reproduction of the pastoral staff that the Holy Father has carried across the globe. This cross is emblematic of his mission to carry the gospel of Jesus Christ to all nations. Secondary images include a stylized Gateway Arch, the Archdiocesan millennium logo and the Fleur de Lis, symbolic of the French heritage of the founders of the City of St. Louis.

Planning a Papal Visit

(Above) The Papal Visit logo features the pastoral staff of Pope John Paul II.

(Right) Left to right— Rev. Henry Breier, Msgr. Richard Stika, Msgr. Ted Wojcicki, Ms. Jennifer Stanard, Msgr. Dennis Delaney and Mr. John Britt.

Within days of the announcement by the Vatican that the Pope would make a Pastoral Visit to St. Louis, Archbishop Rigali had put into place a Planning Committee under the leadership of Msgr. Richard Stika. Joining him were Msgr. Ted Wojcicki, Msgr. Dennis Delaney, Rev. Henry Breier, Ms. Jennifer Stanard, and Mr. John Britt of the United States Secret Service. Immediately, individuals from the community stepped forward with an exuberance and enthusiasm for the Papal Visit.

Honorary co-chairs were named: Mr. August A. Busch III, Sen. John Danforth, Mr. Stan Musial and Dr. Blanche Touhill. From the business and civic community, an executive committee was chosen to lead the effort to plan all aspects of the visit: Rev. Mr. Robert Brooks, Mrs. Hazel Harrison, Mrs. Marie Jeffries, Mr. Jerry Ritter, Mr. Anthony Sansone, Sr. and Dr. Virginia Weldon.

Much work needed to be done. Large meeting spaces had to be reserved and prepared for unique events. Representatives from the city's largest venues, the America's Center and the Kiel Center, remarked on how excited—even honored—they were to be a part of such an historic event.

Committees were formed for Ticketing, Catholic Education, Volunteers, Communications, Hospitality, Hotels, Transportation, Civic Issues, Disability Access, Social Awareness, Music, Ecumenical Greeting, Decor, Printed Materials and Papal Commemoratives, Community Issues, Safety/Security, Fund Raising, Accounting/Finance, Motorcade, Social Awareness and Followup.

All efforts would be directed and coordinated by Mr. Craig Leitner of Contemporary Group of St. Louis for five specific events—a Mass for over 100,000 at the America's Center, a Youth Gathering for 20,000 at Kiel Center, an Evening Prayer Service for 2,000 at the Cathedral Basilica of Saint Louis, and Arrival/Departure Ceremonies at Lambert-St. Louis International Airport. There would also be several motorcades planned so that anyone who wished to see the Pope would have the opportunity.

The Rev. Robert Finn would organize the airport events, and Rev. K. Robert Smoot would plan the "Light of the World" Youth Gathering at the Arch and the indoor event for youth at the Kiel Center. The Evening Prayer Service at the Basilica would be under the direction of Rev. Paul Niemann. Msgr. James Telthorst would oversee the pre-event to the Mass and Rev. James Swift, C.M., would be responsible for one of the largest indoor gatherings ever held anywhere in the United States—the Solemn Eucharistic Celebration.

Whenever the Pope travels the hosting country provides the necessary security arrangements. Directing all the agencies involved, Mr. John Britt of the United States Secret Service and Chief Ronald Henderson of the St. Louis Metropolitan Police Department provided outstanding leadership and a safe trip for the Pope. Their departments were assisted by the Federal Bureau of Investigation, the St. Louis Fire Department, the St. Louis Street Department, the St. Louis County Police Department, the Missouri Highway Patrol, the St. Louis Airport Police and other area law enforcement agencies.

Exuberance and Enthusiasm—"The Pope is Coming!"

Everyone, from the sacristans to the printers responsible for the street banners, was awed by the same thought—the Pope would be here in January. Each task was undertaken with a certain air of disbelief—can this really be happening?

Many hundreds of people, the vast majority of whom were volunteers—priests, religious and laypeople—would spend countless hours in preparation, in meetings, during late nights, looking over budgets, selecting music, tracking down historic chalices, deciding on sweatshirt designs, working with the United States Secret Service, booking hotel rooms and buses, stitching banners…the work would never end. It only would come to a halt on January 26, 1999 when "Shepherd I" landed in St. Louis.

The preparations for each papal event were a complex task of coordinating Archdiocesan plans, Vatican directives, security require-ments and venue logistics. Rev. Robert Finn (center) meets with some of his Arrival and Departure Committee members at the Missouri Air National Guard hangar.

This Pope, the Papacy

The man, Karol Wojtyła, had visited St. Louis once before. In 1969, as the Cardinal Archbishop of Cracow, he visited the local Polish community and celebrated Mass in Polish at St. Stanislaus Kostka Church. Cardinal John Carberry, then the Archbishop of St. Louis, accorded him a warm welcome. The Archdiocesan newspaper, the *St. Louis Review,* observed the event with an article and a photograph. All together it was a low-profile visit, and outside of the Polish community few St. Louisans would have occasion to remember it.

No living St. Louisan will ever forget his visit of January 26-27, 1999. Months of intense organization and preparation preceded the event; the local media gave the

story saturation coverage; and the city all but shut down on the days themselves. There was not even an adequate point of comparison. St. Louis has seen baseball's World Series fifteen times. In 1927 it gave a tumultuous welcome to Charles A. Lindbergh after his historic transatlantic flight. It has welcomed heads of state from other nations. It has thronged to hear the words of countless visiting evangelists. It hosts massive crowds of revelers at its annual riverfront celebration of the July 4th holiday. The Papal Visit, by contrast, was something unique.

The difference between the visit of 1968 and the visit of 1999 was the difference in the office held by the man. Karol Wojtyła returned to St. Louis as Pope John Paul II, the 264th Bishop of Rome, the Successor of St. Peter, the Patriarch of the West, the Supreme Pontiff of the Universal Church. And what a difference. Certainly in the twenty years that he has held the office, he has established his credentials as a respected and even revered world leader. He has shown a magnetism in large crowds that has no parallel, and it is said that he has been seen in person by

(Right) Cardinal Wojtyła in St. Louis, 1969

more people than anyone in history. But St. Louisans and their visitors did not turn out in January to see a celebrity or a performance; they turned out for an encounter with the Vicar of Christ.

The bearer of the office of the papacy is an embodiment of history. He holds an office that is older than the West and seems likely to outlive the West. British historian Thomas Babington Macauley once wrote of it:

> *The proudest royal houses are but of yesterday, when compared with the line of the Supreme Pontiffs. That line we trace back in an unbroken series from the Pope who crowned Napoleon in the nineteenth century to the Pope who crowned Pepin in the eighth; and far beyond the time of Pepin the august dynasty extends, till it is lost in the twilight of fable. The Republic of Venice came next in antiquity, but the republic of Venice was modern when compared with the Papacy; and the republic of Venice is gone, and the Papacy remains… not in decay, not a mere antique, but full of life and useful vigor.*

The papacy remains. Josef Stalin once sneered, "The Pope? How many divisions has he?" Yet Stalin and his whole Communist system in Europe are gone, while the papacy thrives, as Macauley put it, with life and useful vigor.

The history embodied in the office is a conflicted one, and the office is at once both revered and reviled. The papacy is a center of unity and a center of criticism. About it swirl memories of martyrs and saints, rascals and rogues. Its extraordinary claims of primacy and infallibility are a consolation to many and an outrage to others. It is the one office in Christianity that is known to all the followers of Christ, whatever they might think, and few are neutral about what it represents. To some it personifies an inspired story of self-definition and ongoing reform; to others, the propensity for self-delusion and arrogance. It has been a topic of passionate debate for centuries, loved and hated in principle, almost an abstraction. Yet it is an office, not an argument; it continues apace through all the conflict. There is always a Pope; he takes his claims seriously; and by that means he obliges the rest of us to hear him out or to dismiss him.

James Joyce once remarked of the Catholic Church, "Here comes everybody," and in January 1999 they certainly came. There were the faithful, of course: members of the Archdiocese of St. Louis, guests of the Archdiocese, families, parishes, youth groups, religious women and men, deacons, priests, bishops, cardinals. There were the ecumenical and interreligious communities, represented by 95 ministers, rabbis, and other leaders. There were the proud local citizens, Catholic and otherwise: state and civic officials, business persons, the curious, the sympathetic. There was the president of the United States to offer a greeting to a visiting head of state, and the Vice-President of the United

(Above) Saint Louis IX, King of France

Rev. Paul Niemann, director

of the Office of Worship for

the Archdiocese, directed the

plans for the Evening Prayer

Service at the Cathedral

Basilica of Saint Louis. The

Cathedral is known for its

beautiful collection of

mosaics—the largest in

the world.

States to offer a farewell. There were also the detractors: alienated Catholics, religious bigots, street evangelists with hate-filled tracts—their urgency paying homage despite itself.

The eyes of grown men misted as the papal plane touched down. The Pope was in our city. The legendary office, the famous incumbent, the visible representative of Jesus Christ—the Pope was here. It was as if Christ himself were visiting the city, with its potholes and problems, and the city stood up proudly to receive him. There had been so much preparation beforehand: painting, repaving, setting up the barricades. In the middle of the winter, the city was even planting trees. But who would fail to dress up for an honored visitor? And the moment of his arrival was upon us.

White as his robes are, his hair is whiter. His complexion glows. Cameras flash around him as if ignited by his energy. In recent years, as Pope John Paul II has begun to show signs of his age, his appearances are not only impressive, they are touching. His strength and stamina, his command of languages, his ability to work a crowd continue to amaze, but he now moves slowly and with apparent difficulty. His handsome face has lost some of its expressiveness, and his speech is sometimes slurred. For many of his listeners, his situation seems like that of an aging parent, beloved but clearly mortal, and we treasure each day we continue to have him in our midst. This human fragility is also a part of the office. Christ did not put angels at the head of his Church, but men—and these as finite, as passible, and as weak as any of their fellows. Indeed the remarkable thing about the papacy is that Christ has invested such an earthen vessel with such an exalted charge, making clear, as St. Paul taught in another context, that its surpassing value comes from God (see 1 Cor 4:7).

At a deeper level, the excitement of the visit underscored some basic biblical truths. It was necessary for Christ to enter his glory, to pass beyond the cloud, in order to send his Spirit (see Jn 16:7; Acts 1:9). In this way he could transcend the limitations of his own incarnate place in time, to dwell in the hearts of his followers in every age. Yet the cloud itself inspires longing, and the Church in the Spirit calls, "Come!" (Rev 22:17). It is firm Catholic belief that Christ encounters his people both externally and internally, the first in the visible nature of his Church and his sacraments, the second in the gift of the indwelling

Spirit. A papal visit, as an act of the Church's ministry, is designed to celebrate both dimensions of this encounter. Crowds in great numbers gather to see and to hear the Pope, as they would have gathered to see or to hear Christ himself. They come from long distances, they wait for long hours, and when the moment comes, they lean out, they stand on tiptoe, they cheer, they wave, they take photographs to prolong the memory. This is not simply excitement about the appearance of a famous person; this is a longing born of the Spirit, a longing for an encounter with Christ, albeit a mediated encounter.

The Pope himself has a sense of the excitement. He has an actor's training and he knows about presence. He gives himself to a grueling visit schedule of massive liturgies and events, and fills his unscheduled moments with brief private audiences. Before leaving St. Louis, he said to the congregation at the cathedral: "I would have wished to meet personally with each one of the young people at the Kiel Center, and all the many other people at the Trans World Dome and here in the Cathedral Basilica, as well as along the routes and at the airport." Few who heard him would not have wished in kind. But the wish unfulfilled was a statement of its own: longing is the most eloquent of all forms of prayer, and the longing that was highlighted in the context of the Papal Visit continually pointed events beyond themselves. As the Pope slowly mounted the flight stairs for his departure, the overwhelming sense among believers and unbelievers alike was that they had been touched by something spiritual and benign.

For St. Louisans in January 1999 it was a once in a lifetime event.

(Left) Evening Prayer Service, Cathedral Basilica of Saint Louis

The Synod for America

(Above) Solemn Eucharistic
Celebration, Mexico City

Mexico City is a metropolis in the truest sense of the word, one of the largest cities in the world. The capital, the heart of the Mexican nation, has a population of over 15 million. When His Holiness Pope John Paul II arrived there in January of 1999, on a Friday afternoon, over two million spectators lined the motorcade route and gave him a tumultuous welcome. He came to conclude the work of the 1997 Special Assembly for America of the Synod of Bishops, and to present his apostolic exhortation, *Ecclesia in America*, "The Church in America," based on the work of the Synod. Both the meeting and the apostolic exhortation were meant to prepare the 788 million Catholics of the Church in America, a single continent of North and South, to enter the millennium with a new sense of solidarity.

The Pope's message was the Gospel message of peace and life, but it was not abstract sentiment. His apostolic exhortation challenged people to seek conversion, to embrace the mercy of Jesus Christ, and to find communion in service to others. He called on governments to abandon corruption, terror, discrimination and the irrational destruction of the environment. He challenged America to be a beacon of freedom for the world, to stand by those moral truths which are the very heart of its historical experience. He asked Christians to live a life of forgiveness, honesty and transparency of heart.

Mexico had been the first nation that the Pope visited after he was elected in 1978. Twenty years later he returned for a Mass at the Basilica of Our Lady of Guadalupe where he announced a "new springtime of holiness." Cardinals and bishops from throughout the hemisphere, including Archbishop Justin Rigali from St. Louis, a synod delegate, joined the Pope for the four day visit. In a symbolic show of solidarity for the Mass, the flags of all 26 American nations hung in the basilica as Pope John Paul II called for the Church of America to be a "prophetic force against the culture of death."

The fourteen mile ride to the city was a scene that has become as familiar as any in the global media showcase: the sturdy man in his white cassock, the bright white popemobile, the smiling faces of children, the cheers, the waving arms, the yellow and white Vatican flags in the tropical warmth, the multi-colored images of Our Lady of Guadalupe reflecting the midday sunlight, the incessant chant, *"Juan Pablo Segundo!"* Indeed the small children lining the route will be the very ones to realize the promise of his message to promote a new evangelization.

Following the visit to Mexico, Pope John Paul II made a Pastoral Visit to St. Louis. In distinction to the many national tours he has made throughout the world, this would be a brief stopover to greet the people of the Archdiocese of St. Louis and the citizens of the St. Louis region, a very special and relatively intimate visit by the successor of St. Peter to the historic gateway to the American West.

The Pastoral Visit to St. Louis, January 26–27, 1999

Arrival Ceremony

Missouri Air National Guard Hangar
Lambert–St. Louis International Airport
St. Louis, Missouri
January 26, 1999

His Holiness Pope John Paul II was invited to St. Louis by Archbishop Justin Rigali, a personal friend, on repeated occasions since the latter's accession to the See of St. Louis. In April 1998, the archbishop had the pleasure of announcing to the city and the Archdiocese that the invitation had been accepted. It was noteworthy that the visit was to be planned as a pastoral visit to the Archdiocese, not to the nation. Nonetheless, since the Pope is a head of state, he was to be greeted on his arrival in St. Louis by the president of the United States, William J. Clinton.

There were, then, with regard to protocol, two visits. The president, the White House staff, and the government of the United States were providing a state welcome for the Pope. At the same time, the hierarchy of the Catholic Church in the United States, and most especially Archbishop Rigali on behalf of the Archdiocese of St. Louis, were providing a ceremony of pastoral welcome. Each hosting party, the United States government and the Archdiocese of St. Louis, had specific requirements, expectations, and channels of accountability.

Through the ten month course of preparation for the visit, those working with event planners—street departments, police and security details, staging managers, venue operators, liturgical designers, transportation experts, ticket distributors—everyone, had the same energy to go above and beyond the normal call of duty. As the airfield administrator said to Rev. Robert Finn, venue chair for arrival and departure: "If it is possible, we'll get it done. If it is impossible, we'll just take a little longer."

The chosen site for the welcoming ceremony was the hangar of the Missouri Air National Guard at Lambert–St. Louis International Airport. A large, unattractive, cavernous building, it was transformed into a colorful and dignified venue in which leaders of church and government as well as 2300 invited spectators would greet both the president of the United States and the pilgrim Bishop of Rome.

The months of planning beforehand included extensive renovations to the hangar, even the construction of a roadway to make the hangar site more accessible to

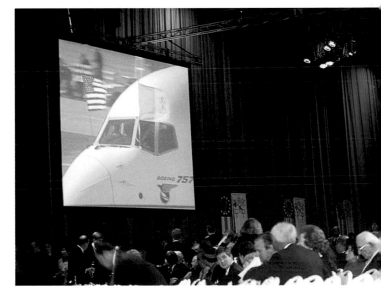

(Below) Shepherd I touches down in St. Louis, January 26, 1999.

nearby Interstate 70, the motorcade route. Because the arrival would be in the dead of winter, there were no outdoor events planned for the arrival. The Holy Father was to leave the plane by an enclosed lift vehicle which would transport him to the National Guard Hangar. Thus sheltered from the elements, he would not be seen by the waiting arrival audience nor by the television audience until he first appeared on the stage that had been prepared to receive him and the president inside the hangar.

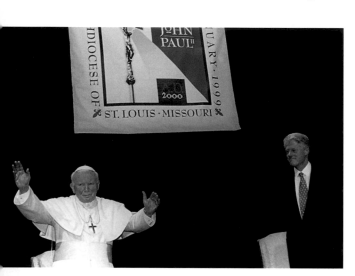

(Above) Pope John Paul II and President Bill Clinton greet those gathered for the Arrival Ceremony.

In advance of his actual arrival, those attending the event at the National Guard Hangar participated in a musical program, viewed videos about the life of Pope John Paul II and listened to Irish performer, Dana, debut her song written for the event using the theme, "that the power of salvation may be shared by all." Behind the scenes, as the crescendo of the day grew intense, event managers, security officers, and St. Louis planners followed their scripts faithfully.

The careful plans and the on-ground logistics for the welcome changed in the blink of an eye. In the moments before exiting the plane the Pope seemed to have decided to make his first appearance in the city in the warm sunshine of an unseasonably spring-like afternoon. Planners, managers, media figures, and security personnel moved decisively. Even the president cheerfully cooperated when asked to move to another part of the arrival site to accommodate the Holy Father's change of plans.

When the door to the Mexicana Airlines jet opened and the Pope descended the staircase to the tarmac, the moment was broadcast on large video screens in the welcoming venue, at Papal Plaza downtown, and in Kiel Center, where the Light of the World Youth Gathering was already in progress. Crowds who had been waiting for hours erupted in applause. The moment was breathtaking. The many, many months of anticipation, the countless hours of planning, the immense effort of so many individuals had come to this simple and powerful moment: the Pope appearing in St. Louis, Missouri, in the bright sunshine of a glorious January day.

When the Pope and his entourage arrived in the hangar, there was sustained excitement and applause. The Pope first greeted the president, and slowly moved through the line of dignitaries on the platform. Security personnel were thorough and access was tight, yet police officers could be seen looking over their shoulders to catch a quick glimpse of the pontiff.

The arrival ceremony opened with the playing of the papal anthem and the national anthem of the United States. The president then welcomed the Pope. "We greet you and we thank you," he said. "For 20 years you have lifted our spirits and touched our hearts." The president noted that this was the Pope's seventh visit to the United States, and commended him for "a boundless physical energy which can only find its source in limitless faith." He honored the Pope "for helping to lead a revolution in Central Europe and the former Soviet Union," also for his work "to bring peace to nations and peoples divided by old hatreds and suspicions." The president then recalled the Pope's challenge to the United States, "to build a society truly worthy of the human person," and reviewed the work of Americans, and Catholic Americans in particular, to meet that challenge. He concluded with the traditional Polish wish, *sto lat I wiecej,* "may you live a hundred years and more," and added his own wish, "May you keep…lighting the way for all of us."

In his own remarks the Pope recalled that the name of St. Louis is forever linked "to the immense human endeavor and daring behind the name, *the Spirit of St. Louis,*" referring to the monoplane in which Charles A. Lindbergh made his famous nonstop solo transatlantic flight in 1927. The Pope then suggested that the upcoming bicentennial of the Louisiana Purchase will be an opportunity to reassert that spirit and "to reaffirm the genuine truths and values of the American experience." At the same time,

(Below) Missouri Governor Mel Carnahan, First Lady Hillary Rodham Clinton and Archbishop Justin Rigali

however, he recalled "times of trial, tests of national character in the history of every country," and the particular time of national trial for America represented by the infamous Dred Scott court decision, whose litigation began in St. Louis. In this decision, the Pope observed, an entire class of human beings, people of African descent, were declared "outside the boundaries of the national community and the Constitution's protection." He went on to note that America faces a similar time of trial today, and challenged Americans to change a culture that still "seeks to declare entire groups of human beings—the unborn, the terminally ill, the handicapped, and others considered 'unuseful'—to be outside the boundaries of legal protection." He concluded that only a higher moral vision could motivate the acceptance of that challenge, and urged the nation to find the values underlying that vision in revering the family as the basic unit of society.

After the welcoming ceremony, the Pope and the president met privately for a short time, and a motorcade took the Pope to the starting point for the first of three tours in the popemobile. From Skinker and Lindell Boulevard, the vehicle followed a parade route east to the archbishop's residence in the Central West End of St. Louis.

"Light of the World" Youth Gathering
Kiel Center
St. Louis, Missouri
January 26, 1999

(Above) Archbishop Justin Rigali welcomes the Holy Father at the "Light of the World" Youth Gathering.

The "Light of the World" Youth Gathering was held at Kiel Center on Tuesday, January 26. Set up and rehearsals began on the previous Sunday and on Monday evening the building was vacated so that the United States Secret Service could begin its security sweep. That work continued through the night into the early Tuesday morning. Only hours before the scheduled opening of the doors at 10:00 a.m., were the production crews allowed to begin staging what was to be an all day event. Speakers needed to do run-throughs. Bands needed to do sound checks. All personnel had to be credentialed, and gift bags for thousands of attendees had to be assembled and distributed. Final rehearsals were completed. The Kiel Center was ready for its long day.

The youth gathering began early Tuesday morning with a one-mile youth march, called Walk in the Light. Tens of thousands of youths participated, arriving from local parishes in Missouri and Illinois, and from places as distant as Massachusetts, Oregon, Texas, Idaho, North Dakota, Nebraska, and Ohio. Their parade route began on the grounds of the Jefferson National Expansion Memorial, beneath the famous Gateway Arch, and proceeded fourteen blocks up Market Street, to a small city park transformed for the occasion into Papal Plaza. "Welcome to the experience of a lifetime," a loudspeaker boomed at the assembly point; "Our Holy Father is coming here to see you." The young marchers responded with enthusiasm and a bouncy fervor.

At the end of the parade route, those with tickets to the indoor event separated to enter the Kiel Center. Others remained outside in the Plaza. Both sites reverberated all day with Christian rock and with testimonies and exhortations. Spirits were high, but the crowds at both venues were well-behaved and orderly. In the Kiel Center and at the nearby Church of St. John

the Evangelist, confessors celebrated the Sacrament of Penance throughout the day with youthful penitents. Hundreds of participants took advantage of the opportunity, soulfully.

Facility managers at Kiel Auditorium said that when the Pope entered the arena it was the loudest outburst they had ever heard. A sense of amazement overwhelmed them as flash cameras kept bursting like fireworks. The seating stands teemed with a life of their own as 20,000 youths waved and shouted and whistled and cried. It was not what you would feel at a crowded rock concert or sporting event. It was an outburst of jubilation—sheer happiness at the sight of the Holy Father. A reporter, in the midst of this wild scene, asked Rev. Robert Smoot, chair of the Kiel event, "How will you quiet this huge crowd to begin your prayer service?" The question was answered when the Pope said, "In the name of the Father…" the familiar words that every child had learned for the beginning of every prayer. And as the Pope made the sign of the cross the Kiel Center fell silent. The prayer service was underway.

The Pope delivered his homily in two parts, the first after the reading and responsorial psalm, the second after the Gospel. In the first part he played on the sports motif of the Kiel Center itself, home to the St. Louis Blues hockey team, the Saint Louis University Billikens basketball team and the St. Louis Ambush soccer team. "Train yourself for devotion," the first reading had just said, in the words of Paul to his younger friend Timothy. The Pope asked his young audience to ask themselves, "What training am I doing in order to live a truly Christian life?" He cited the training that is necessary for competing in the sports played at the Kiel Center, and spoke of "that training that will help you live your faith in Jesus more decisively." He charmed his audience by referring to the excitement of the 1998 home run race of baseball players Mark McGwire and Sammy Sosa, and invited his listeners to feel the same enthusiasm in training for a different goal, "the goal of following Christ, the goal of bringing his message to the world." Later he reminded them, "Even though you are young, the time for action is now!"

In the second part of his homily, the Pope focused on the Gospel theme of the light. "Only if you are one with Jesus," he said, "can you share his light and be a light to the world. Are you ready for this?" He reminded his young listeners of a child's fear of the dark, and spoke of

An inner joy was the principal emotion of the Papal Visit… "not just an inner joy but a jubilation, for the coming of God is also an outward, visible, audible and tangible event" (As the Third Millennium Draws Near, 16).

the darkness of doubt, of loneliness, of violence, of hopelessness. "But you believe in the light!" he stated. "Do not listen to those who encourage you to lie, to shirk your responsibility, to put yourselves first. Do not listen to those who tell you that chastity is *passé*...Do not be taken in by false values and deceptive slogans, especially about your freedom." And developing this idea of freedom, he added a statement of Catholic moral tradition that has become a major theme of his papacy: "Freedom is not the ability to do anything we want. Rather freedom is the ability to live responsibly the truth of our relationship with God and with one another." He concluded: "Remember: Christ is calling you; the Church needs you; the Pope believes in you and he expects great things of you!" His listeners were deeply moved.

Later in the service, he received a group of children, parents, and administrators from Cardinal Glennon Children's Hospital, and gave them a letter to bring back to the hospital community. Still later, on a lighter note, he was presented with a hockey stick and jersey, bearing his name and the numeral "1." Clearly delighted, he announced he would return once more—to play hockey.

Pope John Paul II chooses to spend time with this young flock in just the same way that the pastor of a parish likes to get away from his desk and mix with the kids in his parish. There is a mutually energizing effect. Young people love the Pope because he comes to them with complete sincerity and authenticity. He clearly believes in them, and delivers a message that challenges them to live honestly, to believe in the truth, and to love selflessly. It is a challenge that they accept enthusiastically, both because it calls them to their best and because he witnesses so powerfully by his own example. The Pope, for his part, loves these gatherings of youth. He is relaxed and often playful with them, and deeply appreciates the opportunity to influence the future through them.

The youth also come with a sense of reverence for the universal Church and for the role the papacy plays in that Church. There is little cynicism in the young people who come to a gathering such as this; there is instead a strong yearning to learn more about their faith, to put their faith more evidently in practice, and to make the world a better place by the witness of their own lives. Many of the world's leaders pass the youth by or otherwise fail to connect with them. But the Pope is one leader who does make the effort to connect, and the youth respond to him with liveliness and warmth.

Over 250 bishops were invited to the Youth Gathering and many came. As they arrived in buses and filed in long lines to enter the auditorium, the crowds in the Kiel concourse parted, then pushed forward and applauded. Many young people from around the country, seeing their own bishop, leaned out to greet him and tell him where they were from. Later, during the event itself, many of the bishops warmed the hearts of their young flock by joining the "wave" cheer as it rolled around the circular seating area.

Weeks in advance of the Pope's visit, the St. Louis Cardinals' famous first baseman, Mark McGwire, had been invited to make an appearance at the Youth Gathering and had declined. However, at the last possible moment, word came from the Cardinals organization that he was in town and wanted to meet the Pope. Hasty arrangements were made, and on the concourse just outside of the auditorium itself, he briefly greeted the Holy Father with the traditional gesture of kissing the Ring of the Fisherman. McGwire was as awed as any are on such an occasion, and while the auditorium crowd cheered appreciatively, he waved to the camera carrying the scene.

The Youth Gathering Committee, amidst all the planning, arranging and rehearsing, also took time to manage the weather. Because most of the youths would be outside the Kiel building, weather was a great unknown and a potential problem. While the cloistered religious of St. Louis had been praying for weeks for suitable weather, event planners checked the historical data: January 27, 1996, a low of 38° Fahrenheit; January 27, 1997, a low of 6° Fahrenheit; January 27, 1998, a low of 18° Fahrenheit. This was the Midwest, and it might be quite cold for the Pope's arrival! The balmy weather that actually occurred was attributed to the power of prayer, even in the bemused media.

The Youth Gathering at Kiel Center was unique in many ways and was recognized by Vatican visitors for the competence with which it was put together. It was not only a vibrant gathering of musicians, speakers and preachers, it was also a prayer service led by the Pope. Compared to the World Youth Day Gatherings that attract millions of young people, it was a relatively intimate gathering. This only enhanced its appeal. The chance to see the Pope in this setting, to pray with him, and to experience the infectious joy of the gathering was an experience that few young participants will ever forget.

Solemn Eucharistic Celebration
America's Center
St. Louis, Missouri
January 27, 1999

How splendid he was as he came from within the veil! Vested in his magnificent robes, he ascended the glorious altar, and lent majesty to the court of the sanctuary, his brethren ringed around him like a garland, like a stand of the cedars of Lebanon. Then hymns would re-echo, and over the throng sweet strains of praise resound. All the people of the land would shout for joy, praying to the Merciful One, as the high priest completed the services at the altar. Then coming down he would raise his hands over all the congregation of Israel, the blessing of the Lord upon his lips, the name of the Lord his glory (see Sirach 50:5-20).

The Solemn Eucharistic Celebration at the Trans World Dome was to be the largest indoor event ever held in the United States. Its actual site was America's Center, the name for the complex that comprises both the Trans World Dome and the Cervantes Convention Center. Between them, they would hold almost 110,000 people for the Mass, with participants in the Convention Center viewing the Mass on eight large Jumbotron screens. Event planners would have only 25 hours to prepare the venue, as a previously scheduled automobile show was booked to use the Center until Sunday, January 25th.

In that short period of allotted time, a massive stage was erected for the sanctuary and the musicians, dominated by a 45-foot replica of the Gateway Arch, the internationally recognized landmark emblematic of the city. A 47-foot wooden cross was suspended above the sanctuary, and 4 large Jumbotron screens were placed to televise the liturgy for those in distant seats.

Everyone attending the Mass in the Trans World Dome and the Cervantes Convention Center would have to be in the building by 7:30 a.m. Transportation logistics and a projected dearth of available parking on a business day downtown, meant that waves of buses would deliver people from collections points throughout the metropolitan

area. Some pilgrims got on buses as early as 1:30 a.m. and arrived by 3:30 or 4:00. Everyone who entered the Center for the Mass had to pass through metal detectors, but the long lines were quiet, patient and prayerful.

The Pre-Mass celebrations began at 4:30 a.m., with a video about Pope John Paul II. Morning Prayer began at 5:30 a.m., with the call to worship and the blowing of the traditional Jewish *shofar*—the ram's horn. Several choirs performed, including the Polish Choir of St. Stanislaus Parish, who sang *Bogurodzica,* a hymn to the Mother of God that is one of Poland's oldest national treasures. As the morning prayers continued and the choirs performed, nearly 1000 priests, 500 bishops, and hundreds of religious were arriving at the Dome to take their places in the liturgy.

(Below) Bishops Michael J. Sheridan and Edward K. Braxton, Auxiliaries of the Archdiocese of St. Louis

Despite the massive scale of the arena and the crowd, so unlike a place of worship, the Mass was for many a truly touching experience. Rev. Jim Swift, C.M., who directed the planning of the liturgy said that, from the start and at the direction of Archbishop Rigali, the Mass was carefully choreographed for prayer. No effort would be spared in preparing a place and a plan for reverence and respect for the Eucharist. Bright yellow and white banners covered the advertising signs in the Dome, helping to create a more suitable environment. Bright colored banners hung everywhere, adding an air of festivity. Flowers surrounded the stage, giving it a garden-like appearance. The sound system performed flawlessly and filled the building with praise and worship. The music for the Mass included several pieces commissioned for the Papal Visit, including a rousing Gospel Acclamation. The choirs consisted of 200 adults and 100 children, both of which groups had practiced for months. An elegant orchestral accompaniment enhanced the outstanding beauty of the liturgy.

The man who had traveled to so many other places in the world was about to enter the Trans World Dome in St. Louis. The preparations were complete. People from all walks of life—priests, sound engineers, security agents, laborers, liturgical

The Papal Visit youth orchestra

and choir, under the direction

of Rev. Bruce Forman, included

many members of the

Archdiocese "Young Catholic

Musicians" as well as other

young people from throughout

the St. Louis region.

artists and composers, crane operators, souvenir vendors—had worked for ten months for this moment. Each heart had its own reason. But each heart had the same feeling—joy—exuberant joy at the coming of a man who spoke the truth—"the truth revealed by God."

The first processionals would begin before the Holy Father even left the archbishop's residence in the Central West End. They would include 1500 participants and last nearly 45 minutes. The Pope himself arrived at the Trans World Dome shortly after 9:00 a.m. and toured the Convention Center and the Dome in the popemobile—to loud and sustained cheers. Everywhere could be heard the chant, "John Paul II, we love you."

For Roman Catholics, the Mass, the celebration of the Holy Eucharist, is the principal manifestation of the unity of the Church—the one prayer, the one table, the one bread in which the one Savior is present to his people. Since that unity must always have a visible as well as invisible aspect, the office of the Pope, the servant of the Church's unity, is implied in every Mass. Wherever it may take place in the world, the liturgy of the Mass always prays for the Pope by name. Thus there is a special poignancy to a Mass in which the Pope is not simply implied but actually presiding, actually rendering his service. This was a good part of the excitement of the papal liturgy in St. Louis.

As is the custom of the Bishop of Rome, Pope John Paul II remained seated to deliver his homily at the Mass. His accent was at times a little difficult to understand, but the large video screens used closed captioning to transcribe his words as he spoke them. There was rapt attention to his message. The Pope spoke of the great work of the Archdiocese over many generations, he acknowledged the tremendous sacrifices of the religious congregations of the area, who "have labored for the Gospel with exemplary dedication." He singled out Saint Philippine Duchesne for her holiness and service to the Church, noting for his listeners that, through such figures, "Catholic life has appeared in all its rich and varied splendor. *Nothing less is asked of you today.*"

Echoing the theme of the apostolic exhortation presented in Mexico City, *Ecclesia in America,* "The Church in America," he called for a new evangelism—with a special emphasis on the family and on respect for life. He made a particular appeal for the end to capital punishment, which he said is "both cruel and unnecessary." (Later that day he would make a personal request of the governor of Missouri, Mel Carnahan, to commute the sentence of a man whose execution had been postponed because of the Papal Visit. The next day, despite the prospect of political criticism, Governor Carnahan did exactly that.)

The Pope spoke about the power of the incarnation and its significance for our destiny. He recognized that there may be those who are separated from the practice of their faith. To those, he said, *"Christ is seeking you out and inviting you back...Is this not the moment for you to experience the joy of returning to the Father's house?"* He then spoke of a renewal for all, of a springtime of faith, of hearts filled with generosity and humility, hearts open to the Spirit's purifying grace.

The texts of the liturgy were those assigned for a Votive Mass of the Sacred Heart of Jesus. The theme was the tenderness of God's love for his people. With comfort and affection in his voice, the Holy Father reminded the hundred thousand worshippers in St. Louis and the innumerable viewers throughout the world that, through Jesus, God seeks us out. "Our faith," he said, "is not simply the result of our searching for God. In Jesus Christ, it is God who comes in person to speak to us and to show us the way to himself."

For many participants and television viewers, a highlight of the Mass at the Trans World Dome was the communion rite. Meticulously organized beforehand, it sent hundreds of priests and deacons into the aisles of the stands, each accompanied by an usher bearing a gold and white umbrella. From a distance, the procession of umbrellas

(Above) Rev. James Swift, C.M., chair of the Papal Mass, arrives at the Trans World Dome.

(Left) Archbishop Justin Rigali welcomes the Holy Father before the Eucharistic Celebration.

majestically branching out to every corner of the Dome underlined the Pope's theme of God coming in person to each of us. In a dignified twenty minutes of time, the entire congregation of 110,000 had received communion.

At the conclusion of the Mass, as in all papal appearances, the Secret Service secured the building until the papal entourage departed. It was after noon and most in attendance had been awake since 3:00 or 4:00 a.m. The Mass itself had lasted over two hours. As people left the Dome, an extra edition of the *St. Louis Post Dispatch* was being sold on the street outside, with a full-page, full-color photo of the Pope at the Mass which had just concluded.

The crowds slowly dispersed into the downtown streets around the Trans World Dome, finding the streets largely empty except for the lines of return shuttle buses. Because of the warnings by the police department about traffic snarls and immense crowds, many businesses closed that day, or allowed employees to work at home. As a result, the area in the heart of downtown was deserted. It seemed more like a Sunday than a Wednesday. Some exiting worshippers chose to take cabs or simply to hike out of the area surrounding America's Center. While there was some confusion about bus departure schedules—those who had arrived first during the night were to get the first buses out—many people simply grabbed seats on buses as they continued to roll by designated stops.

The sun was high in the sky; the temperature was approaching 70° Fahrenheit. It seemed as though "the new springtime of faith" that the Holy Father had described in his homily had arrived—literally.

(Right) Auxiliary Bishop Joseph F. Naumann (center) of the Archdiocese of St. Louis and other bishops from Missouri

Evening Prayer Service

Cathedral Basilica of Saint Louis
St. Louis, Missouri
January 27, 1999

The afternoon could be described as balmy. The high temperature was 68° Fahrenheit. It was January 27 in St. Louis, Missouri—not usually a month for mild weather. At 4:30 p.m., nearly 100 ecumenical and interfaith leaders gathered at the Cathedral Basilica of Saint Louis for Evening Prayer.

The end of the Pope's visit was drawing near, and two days of crowds and bustle were drawing to an end. Those at the Cathedral awaited the arrival of the Pope quietly, some prayerfully. One does not usually think of this large building as an intimate space for prayer, but by contrast with the Trans World Dome and the even larger outdoor venues in which the Pope typically appears, a church that seats 2000 is intimate. Those who prayed together with him that evening remember it as prayer.

(Above) Rabbi Robert Jacobs

At the center of the sanctuary stood a pedestal with incense burning, the cantor intoned the antiphon: "Like burning incense Lord, let my prayer rise up to you" (Ps 141: 2). One moment of great drama came when Rabbi Robert Jacobs, at 90, a giant of the local interfaith dialogue, climbed the stairs of the pulpit and read from the prophet Isaiah, first in Hebrew, then in English. This was thought to be the first time that a leader of the Jewish faith had participated in a liturgical celebration presided over by the Pope. It was an idea born in one of the many planning sessions and it was met with great enthusiasm by the Holy Father.

The Pope himself offered a striking image of unity in his homily. Speaking to Jews, Christians, Hindus, Muslims, and representatives of other religious traditions, he stated, "our true mother-tongue is the praise of God, the language of Heaven, our true home." The text of Psalm 67, "Let the peoples praise you, O God; let all the peoples praise you," was sung in a new musical setting specifically commissioned for the Pastoral Visit to St. Louis.

Because of the need to accommodate so many large crowds during the Papal Visit, all of the liturgies and events took place in public arenas. All, that is, except the Evening Prayer Service. The Cathedral Basilica of Saint Louis was the sole consecrated building to be used for any of the celebrations. This magnificent building, when filled with instruments and voices, has a life and energy unlike any other place in the

Archdiocese—indeed the nation. The Romanesque-Byzantine architecture and the intricate artistry of the largest mosaic collection in the world become even more beautiful when they serve as the setting for a celebration such as this. The gold-leafed tesserae and the giant marble columns of the sanctuary seem to shine brighter and stand more majestic. The great bourdon of the organ resounds like thunder, seemingly with the majesty of the divine.

Rev. Paul Niemann, who was responsible for planning the Evening Prayer liturgy, said that when the Cathedral is full—as it is meant to be—the building takes over. The striking beauty of the marble and mosaics, complemented by the musical artistry created for this day, was the remarkable setting for the Pope's closing words, "The Lord is God, the mighty…come then, let us bow down and worship. Amen."

A second moment of drama occurred just after the prayer service as the Pope was leaving. He greeted the vice president of the United States, Albert Gore, Jr. and his wife, and then approached the governor of Missouri, Mel Carnahan. As leader of the worldwide Catholic Church and as a visiting head of state he simply said to the governor, "Show mercy to Mr. Mease." The state of Missouri had scheduled the execution of convicted murderer, Darrell Mease, on that day, but had postponed it because of the Papal Visit. The day after the Pope's departure, Governor Carnahan, citing his respect for the Pope, commuted Mease's sentence to life imprisonment.

At the conclusion of the Evening Prayer Service, the Holy Father sealed the doors to the center aisle of the Cathedral Basilica. The emblem of the Jubilee 2000 Celebration, a color depiction of the world, with the inscription, "Christ yesterday, today, forever" (Hb 13:8), was used as a seal. The doors will remain closed until December 25, 1999, when the celebration of the Great Jubilee, 2000 years of Christian faith, will begin.

The Pope concluded his activities at the Cathedral Basilica by meeting briefly with civil rights heroine Rosa Parks, and then by greeting the crowd outside the building and giving his apostolic blessing.

(Right) Rev. B.T. Rice, chair of the St. Louis Clergy Coalition

Departure Ceremony
Missouri Air National Guard Hangar
Lambert–St. Louis International Airport
St. Louis, Missouri

The Departure Ceremony was brief. It was Wednesday evening. The Holy Father had arrived in Mexico City the previous Friday and had kept a full schedule for six days. Vatican planners were concerned about his stamina and asked that there be as little activity as possible at the Departure. While St. Louisans hoped the Pope would take the podium for a few final words of farewell, he did not. He was not scheduled to speak, and in the end did not even appear on the stage. He made his way through the crowd and greeted many along the way. He received several gifts from the people of the Archdiocese including a spiritual bouquet of prayers from schoolchildren.

The plan was for him to board a lift vehicle to be transported to the Trans World Airlines 767-300 jet waiting just outside the National Guard Hangar. Instead he led the entourage out onto the tarmac and, alone, ascended the flight stairs to the airplane door. Although those who had traveled with the Pope for the past week were concerned that he not overexert himself at the airport, he showed all the world his sheer will to press on. He stopped at the top of the stairs, saluted the city with two hands raised, and disappeared into the aircraft.

The six-year-old nephew of one of the authors was watching the ceremony on television. Like many St. Louisans, he was tired by then, and fell asleep as the Pope mingled with departure well-wishers. He awoke and began crying as the Pope slowly mounted the flight stairs. When his parents asked him why, he said simply, "I miss him already." The city's farewell, though less tearful, was just as heartfelt. At 8:25 p.m., the Trans World Airlines flight, Shepherd I, with His Holiness Pope John Paul II aboard, departed St. Louis for Rome.

More than 1000 priests vested in the early morning hours for the Papal Mass. The community of priests—the sacramental brotherhood— joined together by the hundreds at the Trans World Dome, was a beautiful witness to all who came to worship.

Introduction

The Paths to Conversion, Communion and Solidarity

The Catholic Church in the Archdiocese of St. Louis was blessed beyond measure with the Pastoral Visit of His Holiness Pope John Paul II in January 1999. The local church, as part of the Body of Christ, the universal Church, opened its doors and opened its heart to all to share with all the blessings of faith and the joy of this special visit.

The Pope came to St. Louis to a warm and jubilant reception, in the unblinking eye of media attention. But he came as one of us, as a fellow believer. And the message he brought was one ripe with promise: "The Spirit will truly bring about a new springtime of faith if Christian hearts are filled with new attitudes of humility, generosity and openness to his purifying grace. In parishes and communities across this land holiness and Christian service will flourish if 'you come to know and believe in the love God has for you'" (Homily, Eucharistic Celebration, citing 1 Jn 4:16).

Those who have spent time with Pope John Paul II are impressed by his personal prayer life. They speak of his determination, and they admire his confidence and courage. But even those who have never met him cannot mistake his desire to communicate, to tell all the world about Jesus Christ. The young Polish actor who joined a clandestine seminary during the Nazi occupation of his homeland strode onto the world stage in 1978 when he was elected the 264th successor to St. Peter, the first non-Italian in 456 years.

For the more than 20 years since the night of his election, Pope John Paul II has tirelessly sought to illuminate the lives of all. As the third millennium draws near, Catholics throughout the world thank God that the deposit of 2000 years of faith has been entrusted to this remarkable leader.

Pope John Paul II has been a prolific writer, but even more, an insightful teacher who understands the flock that he tends. As Pope, he has set about to articulate the strength and beauty of the Catholic faith. John Paul II has not been satisfied with condemning the errors of the times, though he has not shrunk from his duty in this regard. Rather he has set about to persuade, and to do so calmly, by the sheer power of the truth and by the consistency of his own witness.

The Catholic Church and the entire metropolitan area of St. Louis experienced an overwhelming joy at the coming of the Pope. But not just the Pope…this Pope.

The Pope's Visit to the American Continent

Just prior to arriving in St. Louis on January 26, 1999, His Holiness Pope John Paul II concluded the Special Assembly for America of the Synod of Bishops, begun in 1997, with the presentation in Mexico City of his apostolic exhortation, *Ecclesia in America,* "The Church in America." The theme of the Special Assembly for America was *The encounter with the living Jesus Christ: The way to conversion, communion and solidarity in America.* This theme is used in the pictorial section of this volume to weave together the photographs taken in St. Louis during the Papal Visit. Various excerpts from the *Catechism of the Catholic Church,* the apostolic exhortation, *Ecclesia in America,* "The Church in America," and the musical and scriptural texts that were used at the papal events in St. Louis are used. Selected quotations are intended to capture the importance of the three main themes of the Holy Father's message for America: conversion, communion, and solidarity. Photo captions have been included to give the reader a reference point with respect to the activities that took place during the Pope's visit to St. Louis. The text of all of the Holy Father's words during the visit are included after the photo essay.

The Holy Father, with an eye on the Great Jubilee of the Year 2000, made clear in his message to America his purpose: a new evangelism. Not a re-evangelization,

but a "new evangelization—new in ardor, methods and expression" (*Ecclesia in America,* 6). It was in the spirit of this evangelism that the Archdiocese of St. Louis selected the theme for the Pastoral Visit of the Holy Father, "To ensure that the power of salvation may be shared by all" (*Tertio Millennio Adveniente,* 16).

"I urge you to let his word enter your hearts, and then from the bottom of your hearts to tell him: 'Here I am Lord, I come to do your will!'" (cf. Heb 10:7)

Pope John Paul II
Homily (Part I), "Light of the World" Youth Gathering

The Path of Conversion
Chapter One

The Path of Conversion

"In this life, conversion is a goal which is never fully attained."

Pope John Paul II
The Church in America, 28

(Above) Volunteer ushers pray during the Papal Mass at the Trans World Dome.

(Page 32) Twenty thousand young people open their hearts to the words of Pope John Paul II at Kiel Center. "…tonight," he said, *"the Pope belongs to you."*

Pope John Paul II, on his seventh visit to the United States, came to St. Louis, inviting all to encounter the living Jesus Christ and to respond to the urgent call to conversion. It was to believers even more than to non-believers that he presented this invitation, since conversion involves a change of heart much more than a change of denomination.

In his apostolic exhortation, *Ecclesia in America,* "The Church in America," he described this conversion as a path. Conversion is not a single dramatic moment in time, but a series of ordinary moments transformed by grace, a path that has been worn by the footsteps of those who have gone ahead of us in following Jesus. It is a way of living, the Pope says, "nurtured through the prayerful reading of Sacred Scripture and the practice of the Sacraments of Reconciliation and the Eucharist" (26). This path of conversion is well worn, but remains unpaved, unperfected.

Conversion, we read in the *Catechism of the Catholic Church,* is an ongoing struggle. The new birth of baptism…has not abolished the frailty and weakness of human nature, nor the inclination to sin. These remain in the Christian life, so that with the help of Christ's grace we may prove

ourselves in the struggle, an effort of conversion directed toward holiness and eternal life (see 1426).

In his letter *Ecclesia in America,* the Pope says that in this new life, prayer, guided by the Holy Spirit, enables us little by little "to recognize God in every moment and in everything; to contemplate God in every person; to seek his will in all that happens" (29). The Holy Father, using the parable of the lost sheep in his homily at the Solemn Eucharistic Celebration in St. Louis, offered encouragement to all who wander from the path: "God's love," he said, "is a love that searches us out. It is a love that saves. This is the love that we find in the Heart of Jesus" (Homily, Eucharistic Celebration).

This is the path that we seek, the Path of Conversion. Its story of sin and redemption, captivity and freedom—the great turning point of a universal saving history—was retold and celebrated in the events of the Pastoral Visit to St. Louis in January 1999.

(Above) Pope John Paul II, at the Solemn Eucharistic Celebration at the Trans World Dome, listens to the words of Luke's gospel: "...the Pharisees and scribes began to complain, saying, 'This man welcomes sinners and eats with them'" (Lk 15:2).

(Left) A young Vietnamese American couple presents the wine and water at the Papal Mass.

John Paul II

(Right) Left to right—Bishop Boland, Bishop Leibrecht and Bishop Gaydos, all bishops of the Missouri Province, listen attentively to Pope John Paul II at the "Light of the World" Youth Gathering.

(Above) Pope John Paul II enters the Trans World Dome to Palestrina's *Tu es Petrus,* sung in Latin. "Behold a great priest, who in his days pleased God."

(Opposite Page) A sign language interpreter leads the hearing impaired in the Evening Prayer Service: "I have called to you, Lord; hasten to help me!" (Ps 141)

"...an invitation to respond readily to Christ
with a more decisive personal conversion
and a stimulus to ever more generous fidelity
to the Gospel."

Pope John Paul II
The Church in America, 26

Electricians, laborers and

stagehands worked through

the night of January 26 to

prepare the Trans World Dome

for the arrival of the Pope.

The Papal Mass was the

largest indoor gathering ever

held in the United States.

John Paul II

(Below) The Holy Father receives the offertory gifts at the Papal Mass. "Lord, look on the heart of Christ your Son filled with love for us. Because of his love accept our Eucharist and forgive our sins" (Preparation Rite).

(Right) In response to the incessant prayers of the nine communities of contemplative sisters, the Lord blessed visitors to St. Louis with a spring-like day and a high temperature of 68° Fahrenheit.

(Opposite Page) In the afterglow of a beautiful day, prayers fill the Cathedral Basilica of Saint Louis. "Those whom the Lord has ransomed…will meet with joy and gladness, sorrow and mourning will flee" (Is 35:10).

Msgr. Richard Stika served as general chair of the The Papal Visit Committee. John Britt (left), United States Secret Service and Craig Leitner (far right) of Contemporary Group worked long days at the Catholic Center.

(Right) The Holy Spirit Adoration Sisters (the Pink Sisters) left their cloister, Mt. Grace Convent in north St. Louis, to attend the Papal Mass. Consecrated religious who choose a vow of stability—to stay in one place—are rarely permitted to go outside their community.

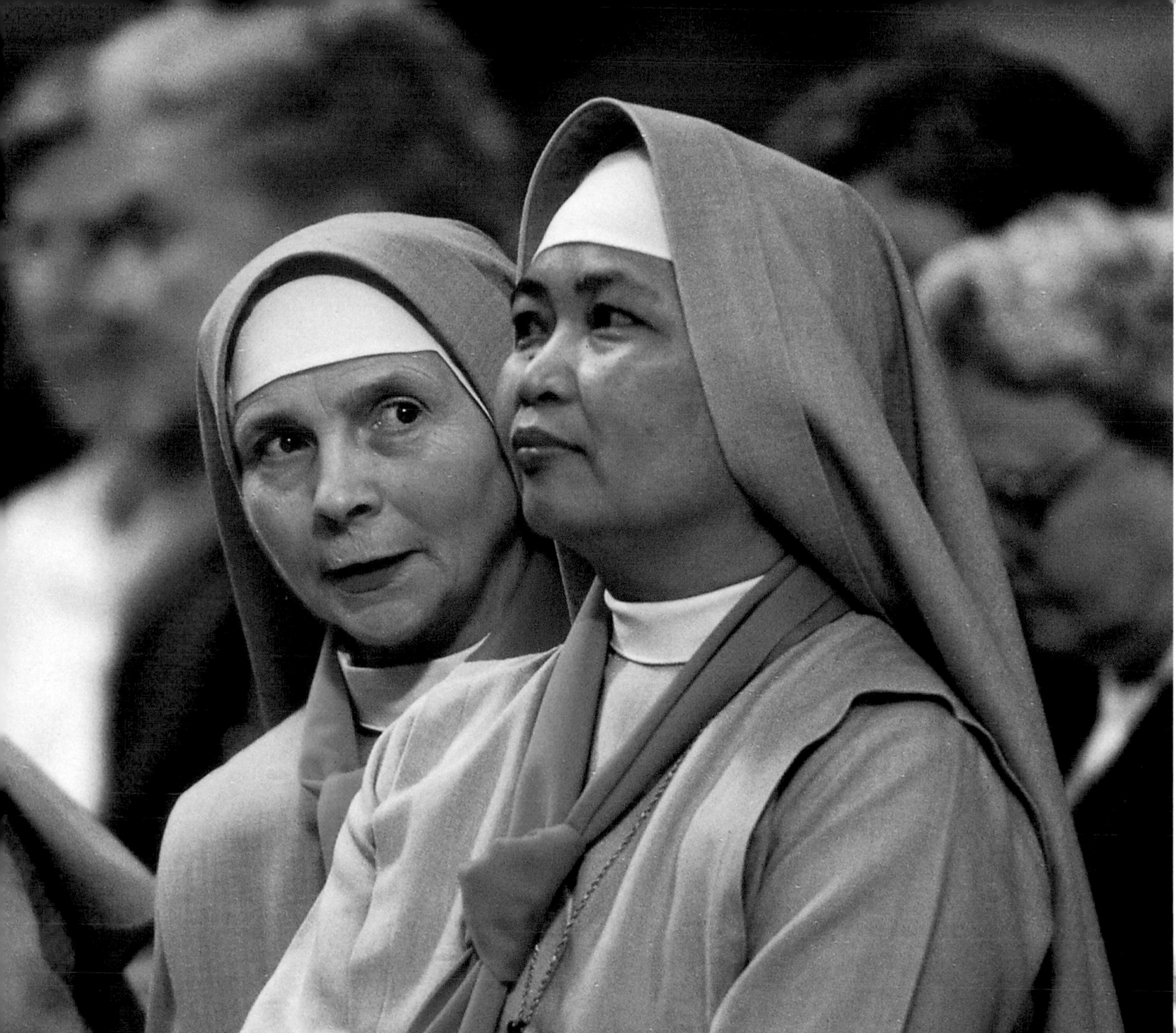

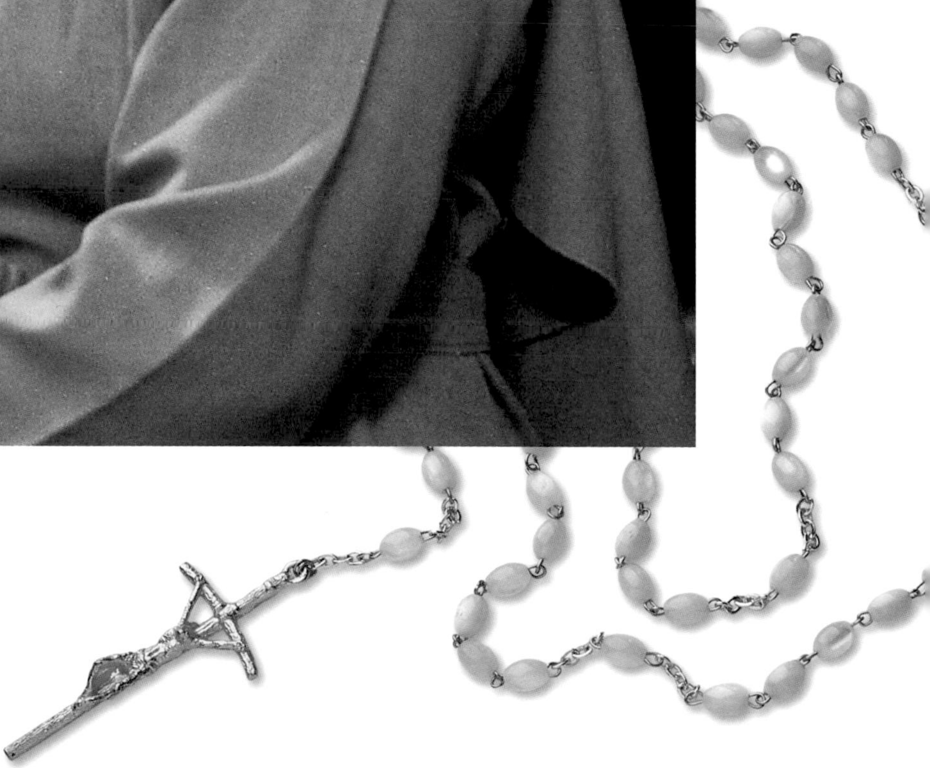

(Left) As the Pope's motor-cade approaches the Kiel Center, thousands watch inside on the Jumbotron and sing, "We are holy, we are strong! Cry the gospel, cry the gospel with your life!"

(Below) At the Evening Prayer Service, Pope John Paul II leads the community: "The Prophet's message is a *call for trust,* a call to courage, a call to hope for salvation from the Lord. 'Be strong, fear not! Here is your God…he comes to save you'" (Is 35:3-4).

Mr. Steve Mamanella of the Office of Communications for the Archdiocese coordinated media relations for one of the largest gatherings of the media ever in St. Louis. Over 2,500 media credentials were issued.

"…the Prophet Isaiah envisions a people returning from exile, overwhelmed and discouraged. We too sometimes experience the parched desert-land: our hands feeble, our knees weak, our hearts frightened."

Pope John Paul II
Homily, Evening Prayer Service

(Left) A youthful St. Louis
smile bids a fond farewell at
the Departure Ceremony.

(Right) Twenty thousand sit in silence straining to listen to the Pope's remarks as a lone voice from the crowd shouts "Viva il Papa" (long live the pope). After a thunder of applause and a long theatrical pause, the Holy Father, in jest, reprimands the young person.

(Opposite Page) Clergy of the Archdiocese in the sanctuary of the Cathedral Basilica of Saint Louis pray with the successor to St. Peter: "O God come to my assistance. Lord make haste to help me" (Ps 141:1).

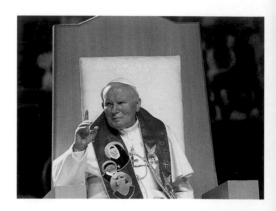

(Right) After a ten-hour day of music, witness, prayer and reconciliation, young people applaud the Pope as he comes to the stage at Kiel Center.

"Remember: Christ is calling you; the Church needs you; the Pope believes in you and he expects great things of you!"

Pope John Paul II
Homily (Part II), "Light of the World" Youth Gathering

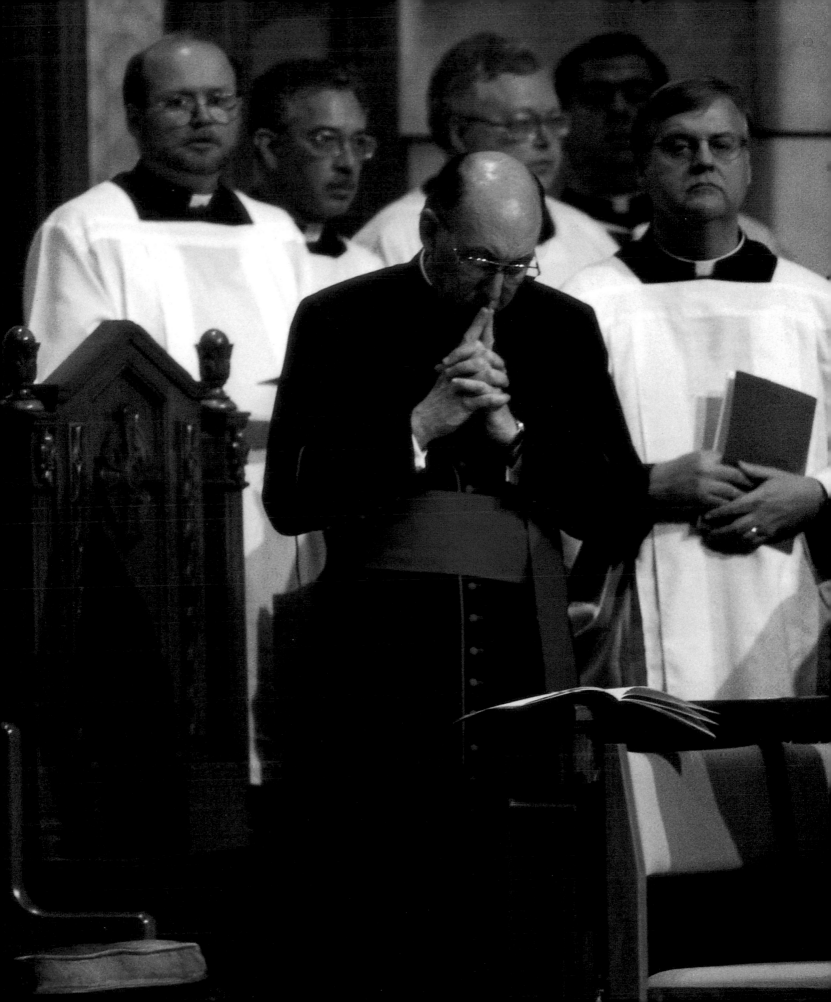

Hundreds of police officers

could be seen at each papal

event. Hundreds more Secret

Service and FBI agents worked

both inside and outside the

venues. Nearly 2,500 media

credentials were issued to

local, national and international

news organizations. Inside

this tight circle of security,

under the bright television

lights, ordinary people prayed,

applauded, cheered and cried.

(*Above*) Surrounded by Secret Service agents and followed by an armored car, the missionary of peace enters the Trans World Dome. "I was glad when they said unto me: we will go into the house of the Lord" (Ps 122:1).

(*Opposite Page*) An ecstatic sister views the Holy Father's arrival on the Jumbotron at America's Center.

"I sought the Lord, and he answered me, delivered me from all my fears."

Ps 34:5

"*In all my travels I tell the world about your youthful energies and your readiness to love and serve.*"

Pope John Paul II
Homily (Part I), "Light of the World" Youth Gathering

John Paul II

(Right) The striking Cathedral Basilica of Saint Louis serves as the setting for the Evening Prayer Service. The Canticle of Mary was set to a new composition, commissioned for the Pastoral Visit: "The Almighty has done great things for me, and holy is his Name" (Lk 1:49).

(Pages 52 and 53) "Light of the World" Youth Gathering, Kiel Center

(Opposite Page) At the Rite of Commissioning, Pope John Paul II blesses a young woman: "Receive the sign of the cross on your eyes that you may see the glory of God."

(Above) The popemobile passes the Cathedral Basilica of Saint Louis on the last of three motorcades in St. Louis.

(Right) A well-equipped visitor stands ready to capture the papal memories on film.

"Mr. President, dear friends…I know that you will hear my plea to open wide your hearts to the ever increasing plight and urgent needs of our less fortunate brothers and sisters throughout the world."

Pope John Paul II
Remarks, Arrival Ceremony

(Above) Some of those honored to participate during the Papal Mass as readers, presenters of the gifts and communicants wait for the arrival of the Pope.

(Right) Pope John Paul II, President Clinton and Archbishop Rigali at the Arrival Ceremony.

(Opposite Page) A 45-foot model of the Gateway Arch frames the crest of Pope John Paul II—the cross symbolizing Jesus and the letter "M" representing Mary.

(*Left*) Eleven American cardinals and three from the Vatican join Pope John Paul II, Vatican Secretary of State Cardinal Sodano and Archbishop Rigali at the Cathedral Basilica of Saint Louis for the Evening Prayer Service.

(*Pages 62 and 63*) Musicians Tom Booth and Steve Angrisano lead the singers on stage, the 500-voice papal youth choir, and the entire "Light of the World" Youth Gathering in songs of praise.

The papal events were rousing celebrations. Music helped make them so. Singers, cantors, musicians, directors and composers worked tirelessly to make the Pastoral Visit of Pope John Paul II to St. Louis most memorable. Several new musical settings were commissioned by the Archdiocese for the visit.

"*The encounter with the living Jesus impels us to conversion.*"

Pope John Paul II
The Church in America, 26

Priests wait backstage for the

beginning of the Papal Mass

in new vestments made for

the Pastoral Visit. Over 1,500

clergy concelebrated with

their brother priest, Pope

John Paul II.

(Below) Students traveled great distances to St. Louis, even without tickets to the events, just to be with other young people—to watch and to pray.

(Opposite Page) Pope John Paul II and Archbishop Rigali pass through the crowd at Kiel Center. Nearly 20,000 young people attended the "Light of the World" Youth Gathering.

*"In this is love: not that we have loved God, but that he loved us
and sent his Son as expiation for our sins."*

1 Jn 4:10

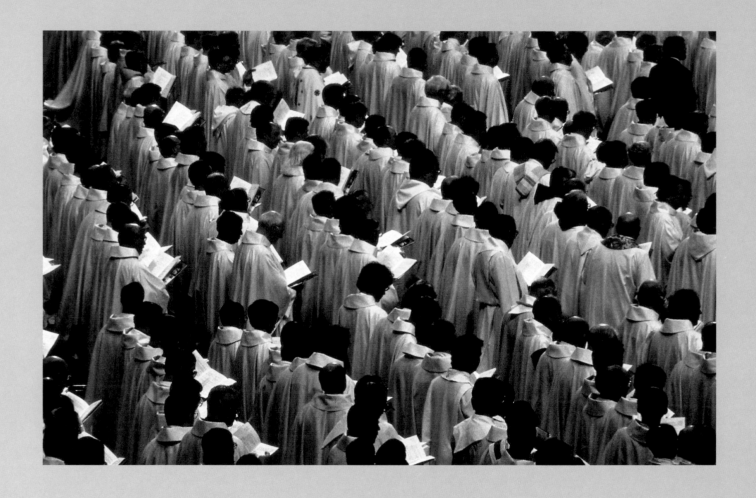

"*A special greeting to the Priests, who carry forward with love the daily pastoral care of God's people.*"

Pope John Paul II
Words at the end of Mass, Eucharistic Celebration

The Path to Communion

Chapter Two

The Path to Communion

"As you, Father are in me and I in you,
may they also be one in us."

Jn 17:21

This is Jesus' plain and simple wish for us: to be united with God. Catholic Christians find this unity, this communion in the Eucharist.

In his letter, *Ecclesia in America,* "The Church in America," Pope John Paul II describes the Eucharist as "the outstanding moment of encounter with the living Christ." He asks pastors "to give the Sunday Eucharistic celebration new strength, as the source and summit of the Church's life" (35). Everyone, he says, is invited and encouraged to participate actively and worthily in this communion. In this act, through communion with Christ, we enter into communion with all believers.

He also makes clear that the lay faithful are the leaven in the loaf. "The renewal of the Church in America will not be possible," he says, "without the active presence of the laity. Therefore, they are largely responsible for the future of the Church" (44). The Church is the "sign and instrument of the communion willed by God, begun in time and destined for completion in the fullness of the Kingdom" (33).

(Above) Hundreds of ciboria were prepared for Mass and contained 110,000 Communion hosts.

(Page 66) Over 1000 priests concelebrate at the Papal Mass, January 27, 1999.

John Paul II at the same time acknowledges a divided world, where countries, states, communities and families suffer brokenness and violence.

Often it is difficult to see signs of oneness and wholeness in our midst. Yet families are to be "the sanctuary where life is born and welcomed as God's gift" (46). The conjugal relationship between husband and wife is "a relationship which, between Christians, is sacramental" (46). Communities, often disturbed by "corruption, terror, racial discrimination, inequalities and the irrational destruction of nature" (56) must foster leadership that embodies values such as "mercy, forgiveness, honesty, transparency of heart and patience" (44). He points to the source of division among nations: a foreign debt which suffocates development and an arms race that paralyzes the progress of peoples. In the face of these divisions, the Holy Father implements the scriptural task of "feeding the entire flock of Christ" (Jn 21:15-17).

The Pope concludes: "With serene trust in the Lord of history, the Church prepares to cross the threshold of the Third Millennium freed from prejudice, hesitation, selfishness, fear or doubt, and convinced of the fundamental and primary service which she must provide as a testimony to her fidelity to God and to the men and women of the continent" (75).

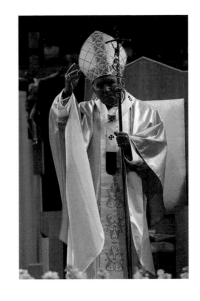

(Above) Pope John Paul II greets the assembly at the Trans World Dome, January 27, 1999.

"Take this, all of you, and drink from it: this is the cup of my Blood."

Eucharistic Prayer

(Left) Thousands of flash-bulbs fill the Trans World Dome as a devout silence falls over the assembly. Pope John Paul II at the consecration of the wine, raises the same chalice that was used 300 years earlier at the first masses celebrated in what is now St. Louis.

(Below) Worshippers gather at the Cathedral Basilica of Saint Louis for the Evening Prayer Service.

(Opposite Page) One of several families presenting the offertory gifts to the Holy Father.

(Below) Vice President and Mrs. Gore, and Governor and Mrs. Carnahan join the interfaith community at the Evening Prayer Service.

The "Light of the World" Youth Gathering included live music and activities throughout the day outside of Kiel Center at "Papal Plaza," a seven-square-block area of downtown St. Louis. Visitors could find everything from pretzels to papal flags.

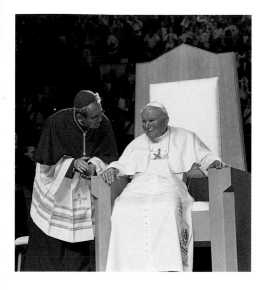

(Left) Archbishop Rigali with his longtime friend at the "Light of the World" Youth Gathering, Kiel Center.

(Below) St. Louis Cardinal baseball star Mark McGwire meets with Pope John Paul II backstage at Kiel Center.

(Opposite Page) Children in the brisk January morning await the Holy Father's motorcade in the city's Central West End.

"*Send forth your spirit, O Lord, and open our heart to your Word; and you will renew the earth!*"

Gospel Acclamation, Michael Joncas
"Light of the World" Youth Gathering

"...Eucharist...the outstanding moment of encounter with the living Christ...the source and summit of the Church's life."

Pope John Paul II
The Church in America, 33

(Pages 76 and 77) In the blazing morning sun the "Walk in the Light" youth walk moves west on Market Street in downtown St. Louis.

(Right) The Pope's motorcade approaches the Kiel Center in downtown St. Louis for the "Light of the World" Youth Gathering.

(Opposite Page) Pope John Paul II distributes Communion to a few of the 110,000 worshippers. "Happy are those who are called to his supper" (Communion Rite).

Rabbi Robert P. Jacobs,

who read from Isaiah at the

Evening Prayer Service, joins

the ecumenical and interfaith

congregation in song. Never

before had a rabbi participated

in a papal liturgy, making it

an historic event for St. Louis

and the Church.

(Right) Fifty reconciliation stations were set up at the "Light of the World" Youth Gathering in Kiel Center. "…the Holy Spirit works ceaselessly to create communion and to restore it when it is broken."

(Below) Throughout the day Papal Plaza in downtown St. Louis was filled with music, witnessing and preaching.

"*We must proclaim that this communion is the magnificent plan of God the Father.*"

Pope John Paul II
The Church in America, 35

(Above) Pope John Paul II
leads 20,000 young people
in the Rite of Commissioning
at the Kiel Center.

(Pages 82 and 83) In his homily at the "Light of the World" Youth Gathering, the Pope challenged young people to believe in the light, to be chaste, to choose freedom.

(Left) One of the many prayerful moments during the "Light of the World" Youth Gathering at Kiel Center.

(Opposite Page) Seminarians and the deacon, raising high the Word of God, lead the Entrance Processional at the Papal Mass.

(Below) The Holy Father and the Vatican Members of the Papal Party are greeted by President Clinton as they arrive in St. Louis from Mexico City.

(Right) Irish singer Dana entertains guests at the Arrival Ceremony at the airport.

(Above) Liturgical dance performers open the "Light of the World" Youth Gathering.

(Right) These young people begin their day with 20,000 others at the Gateway Arch for the "Walk in the Light" youth walk to Kiel Center.

(Below) The facade of the Cathedral Basilica of Saint Louis, bathed in television lights, provides a dramatic backdrop for Pope John Paul II's farewell to the citizens gathered outside.

"The Church is the sign of communion because her members, like branches, serve the life of Christ, the true vine." (cf. Jn 15:5)

Pope John Paul II
The Church in America, 33

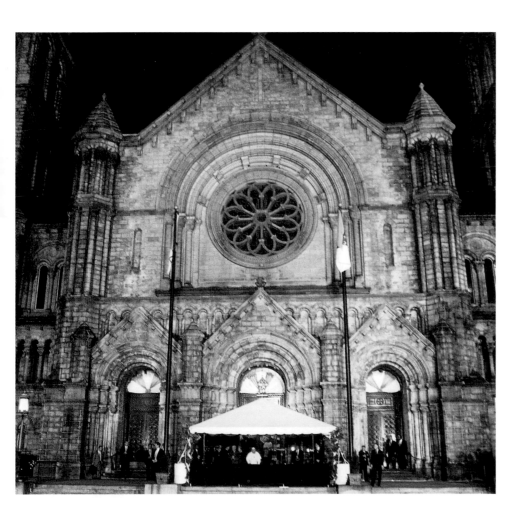

More than 8,000 individuals—typically faithful Catholic parishioners—volunteered to carry out the endless tasks at each of the papal venues. Everyone was overjoyed at having the chance to take part in the project. Several of the ushers at the Cathedral Basilica revel in the moment.

(Left) Transportation logistics were one of the many challenges facing the planners who moved tens of thousands of people in and out of the various venues.

Enthusiastic. Astonished.

Graceful. Awed. Just a few of

the words that might describe

the local and national media

who covered the Papal Visit

to St. Louis. Rev. K. Robert

Smoot is interviewed at the

"Light of the World" Youth

Gathering which he organized.

(Below) Ushers disperse throughout the Trans World Dome. Their bright gold and white umbrellas serve as locators for Communion stations.

(Opposite Page) Special guests selected to receive Communion from Pope John Paul II arrive at the Trans World Dome for Mass.

"…there is one Lord, one Body and one Bread, one great commandment, one great Communion…"

Richard Proulx, "Though We Are Many," sung during Communion at the Papal Mass

(Opposite Page) Two of the hundreds of consecrated religious join the Holy Father in the Eucharistic Celebration. "The bread of angels becomes the bread of man, the heavenly bread gives an end to earthly forms" (Panis Angelicus).

(Below) Pope John Paul II is greeted by the mayor of St. Louis, Clarence Harmon, and his wife.

(Right) Just days before the Papal Visit, St. Louis experienced an ice storm. The wintery weather broke into a few balmy days for the Pope's visit.

"As you, Father, are in me and I in you, may they also be one in us."

Jn 17:21

(Above) The bread and wine that will become the Body and Blood of Christ at the Papal Mass.

(Right) Pope John Paul II opens the sacred liturgy for 110,000 worshippers at America's Center.

(Pages 96 and 97) The processional banners at the Papal Mass represent the rivers symbolic of both the St. Louis region and the water of baptism that brings us a new life in God.

(Above) Crushing crowds filled every venue in which the Holy Father appeared. However, compared to many of the outdoor liturgies and events at which the Pope has presided through-out the world, St. Louisans enjoyed relatively intimate settings in which to see the Pope and pray with him.

John Paul II

"Solidarity is thus the fruit of the communion which is grounded in the mystery of the triune God, and in the Son of God who took flesh and died for all."

Pope John Paul II
The Church in America, 52

The Path to Solidarity

Chapter Three

The Path to Solidarity

"By this all will know that you are my disciples,
if you have love for one another."

Jn 13:35

(Above) The bright smiles of these young sisters match the bright afternoon sun as they await the Holy Father's arrival at the Cathedral Basilica of Saint Louis.

This one simple act, love for one another, is the mark of the Christian community. Each person, acting upon his faith, lives out the life that Christ has given to him. Christians do this within the community; they celebrate it in the Eucharistic gathering. Pope John Paul II, in his letter *Ecclesia in America,* "The Church in America," envisions global solidarity in this love. He describes a world in which believers cannot fail to witness ardently to the truth that is Jesus Christ, a world in which Christians are to be living beacons of faith, hope and charity (see 53).

While the Eucharist is "the living and lasting center" around which the Church gathers (n. 35), the love of Christ as lived out in the world is the path of solidarity. All people share the image and likeness of God, and this fact alone serves as a basis for commonality and solidarity. It makes man "God's masterpiece" (57).

The Holy Father describes a world—as the third millennium draws near—with its increasing globalization of culture, a phenomenon too often characterized "by the loss of a sense of God and the absence of those moral principles which should guide the life of every person" (56). Crossing the threshold of the new millennium, John Paul calls for universal solidarity and a commitment to the Gospel, the culture of life. Such a culture will recognize the dignity of each individual person and strive to ensure that no one is marginalized. Solidarity, the Pope says, "is expressed in Christian love which seeks the good of others, especially of those most in need" (52).

Recognizing America's global leadership and economic influence, the Pope calls for an "economic order dominated not only by the profit motive but also by the pursuit of the common good" (52). In his letter *Ecclesia in America*, he describes a scene of poverty, drugs, corruption, torture, and environmental waste, and in the face of these disasters, he calls the Church to lead in America on the basis of God-given strengths.

Our conversion, our baptism, our communion affirms our solidarity not only with other believers, but with all humanity created in the image and likeness of God. The Gospel way of life "leads to the service of our neighbors in all their needs, material and spiritual, since the face of Christ shines forth in every human being" (52).

When the Pope was in St. Louis, he said, "America will remain a beacon of freedom for the world as long as it stands by those moral truths which are the very heart of its historical experience. And so America: If you want peace, work for justice. If you want justice, defend life. If you want life, embrace the truth—the truth revealed by God" (Homily, Cathedral Basilica of Saint Louis).

(Above) Archbishop Rigali welcomes the Holy Father to the Cathedral Basilica of Saint Louis.

(Page 100) Over 200 area students performed as the papal youth choir at the Kiel Center.

"Our prayer this evening reminds us that our true mother-tongue is the praise of God..."

Pope John Paul II
Homily, Evening Prayer Service

(Left, Top) Archbishop Rigali introduces the leadership of the Church in the United States at the Arrival Ceremony.

(Left, Bottom) Hours of anxious anticipation precede the Holy Father's arrival for Mass.

(Opposite Page) The cantor leads the people in song. "Like burning incense, Lord, let my prayer rise up to you" (Ps141:2).

Dr. John Romeri (right, at rehearsal) selected several new compositions for the Papal Visit and conducted members of the orchestra and a 200-voice choir for the Papal Mass at the Trans World Dome.

(Right) At the conclusion of the Papal Mass, the Holy Father says farewell to the crowd which fills the Trans World Dome with a thunderous applause.

(Pages 108 and 109) The old and the young, the weak and the strong pray with their shepherd, Pope John Paul II.

"Though we are many, in Christ we are one."

Richard Proulx, Communion Song, Eucharistic Celebration

(Above) Visitors scan the
crowd as they wait for the
Holy Father's arrival at the
Trans World Dome.

"Mr. President, dear friends: I am pleased to have another opportunity to thank the American people for the countless works of human goodness and solidarity..."

John Paul II
Remarks, Arrival Ceremony

(Left, Top) Pope John Paul II addresses those attending the Arrival Ceremony. "...the spirit of compassion, concern and generous sharing— must be part of the *'Spirit of St. Louis.'"*

(Left, Bottom) Archbishop Justin Rigali greets the Holy Father at the "Light of the World" Youth Gathering.

(Below) Pilgrims from as far away as the west coast line the many miles of motorcade routes.

(Opposite Page) Pope John Paul II repeats the words of Jesus and every other priest at the Consecration: "This is my body."

"Beloved, if God so loved us, we must also love one another."

I Jn 4:11

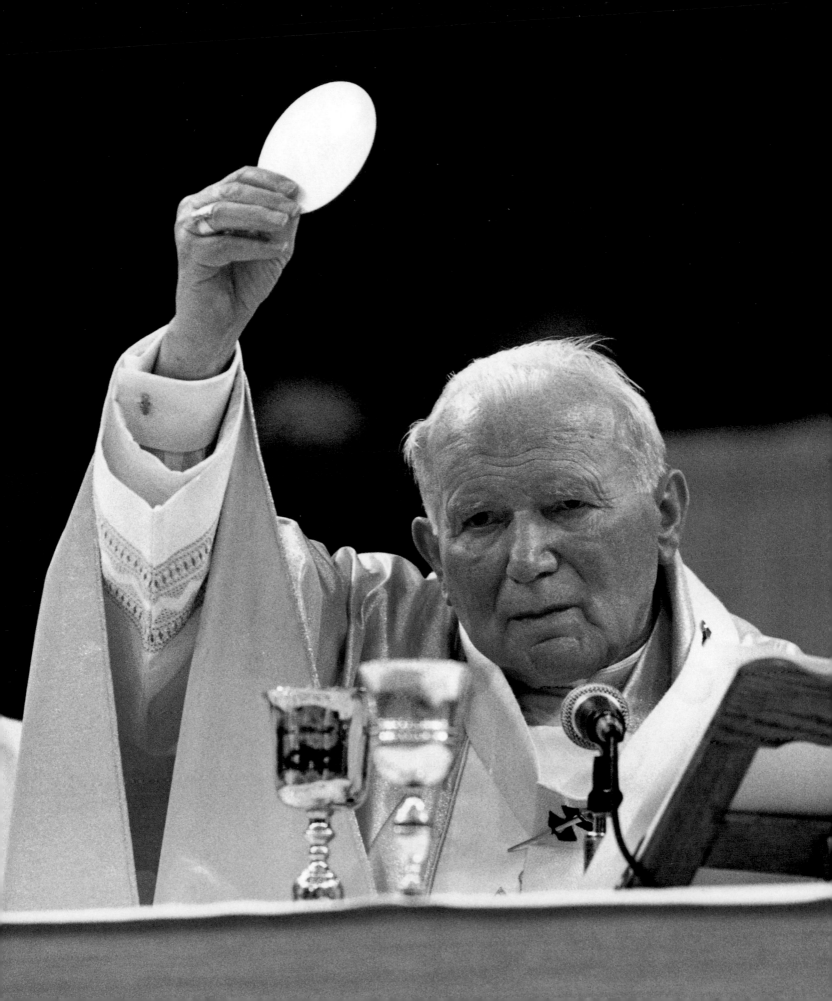

(Left) Pope John Paul II, near the end of his six-day trip to the Americas, strains to move about during the Papal Mass.

(Above) The Trans World Dome—a 60,000-seat sports arena—was skillfully transformed overnight into a one-day cathedral for the Papal Mass.

(Opposite Page) Every one of St. Louis' numerous religious communities was represented at the Papal Mass.

"In this area [St. Louis], numerous Religious Congregations *of men and women have labored for the Gospel with exemplary dedication."*

Pope John Paul II
Homily, Eucharistic Celebration

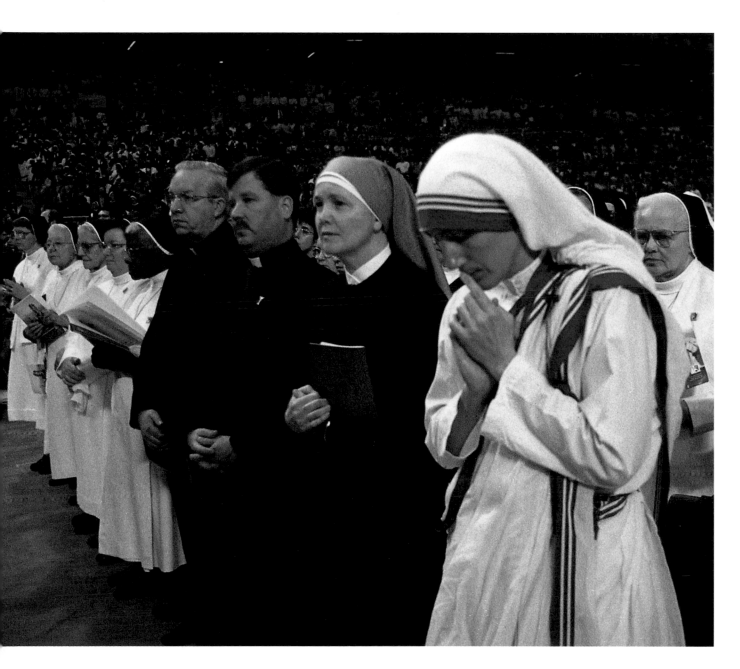

(Above) Well before dawn, buses by the hundreds pick up those attending the Papal Mass. Some boarded as early as 1:30 a.m.

(Opposite Page) The "Walk in the Light" youth walk begins on the grounds of the Gateway Arch even before the Holy Father's plane leaves Mexico City.

"Young friends, in the days and weeks and years ahead, for as long as you remember this evening, remember that the Pope came to the United States, to the City of St. Louis, to call the young people of America to Christ, to invite you to follow him."

Pope John Paul II
Homily (Part II), "Light of the World" Youth Gathering

Dozens of young religious women took part in the Youth Gathering at Kiel Center. Thrilled, nervous, excited... emotions of anticipation ran through this crowd backstage. During his homily the Pope, in the words of St. Paul, told the crowd to "train yourself for devotion" (1 Tim 4:7).

(Right) Children display their rally handkerchiefs with the Papal Visit logo as they await the arrival of the Pope's motorcade.

(Pages 120 and 121) Motorcycle officers from the St. Louis Metropolitan Police Department, the St. Louis County Police Department and the Kansas City Police Department secure the area along Lindell Boulevard prior to the Pope's arrival.

"As morning breaks I look to you: I look to you, O Lord, to be my strength this day." (Ps 63)

Hymn, Michael Joncas
Morning Prayer, Trans World Dome

Workers prepare to raise into

place a 47-foot wooden cross

at the Trans World Dome.

The altar was designed by

Angelo Gherardi, a renowned

liturgical artist who is a

resident of Chicago and a

native of Italy.

(Opposite Page) Many people expended great effort to be a part of the papal events.

(Above) All area Catholic schools and St. Louis City public schools closed to allow the large crowds easier access to the venues and to free up the buses needed to transport tens of thousands of participants.

(Opposite Page) In the afterglow of the Papal Mass, priests await instructions from security officials for leaving the Trans World Dome.

(Right, Top) A simple sentiment on a bed sheet banner greets the Holy Father along Lindell Boulevard.

(Right, Bottom) Pope John Paul II, always in good humor, tries on a sombrero given to him by the press corps aboard Shepherd I as he departs Mexico.

"Taking the Gospel as its starting-point, a culture of solidarity needs to be promoted…"

Pope John Paul II
The Church in America, 52

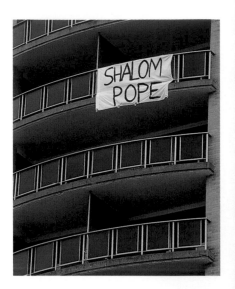

John Paul II

(Right) The Adoration
Sisters of the Holy Spirit—
"the Pink Sisters"—became
the improbable media
darlings of the Papal Visit.

(Above) Pope John Paul II greets a family during the Preparation Rite at the Papal Mass.

(Opposite Page) Young visitors enjoy the pleasant weather and fast food along the papal motorcade route.

(Pages 130 and 131) Tens of thousands rejoiced in and around the papal venues.

"Only a higher moral vision can motivate the choice for life. And the values underlying that vision will greatly depend on whether the nation continues to honor and revere the family..."

Pope John Paul II
Remarks, Arrival Ceremony

When this Pope travels, the national and international media follow. More than 2,500 media credentials were issued. A cable network technician works backstage at the Missouri Air National Guard hangar prior to the arrival of the Holy Father's plane from Mexico City and the President of the United States.

"…the face of Christ shines forth in every human being."

Pope John Paul II
The Church in America, 52

(Below) Representatives of the ecumenical and interfaith communities are greeted by the Holy Father at the Cathedral Basilica of Saint Louis.

(Right) One of the many consecrated religious who came to catch a glimpse of the Holy Father.

(Opposite Page) Pope John Paul II blesses the crowd as he departs St. Louis. He surprised everyone by ignoring the mechanical "people mover" and energetically walking up the long flight of stairs to board the Trans World Boeing 767, Shepherd I, for his trip back to Rome.

"*I will always remember St. Louis. I will remember all of you. God bless St. Louis! God bless America!*"

Pope John Paul II
Final Words, Evening Prayer Service

Transcripts of the Words of His Holiness Pope John Paul II in St. Louis

Arrival Ceremony

Lambert–St. Louis
International Airport
Missouri Air National Guard

Remarks

Dear People of St. Louis, dear People of the United States,

1. It is a great joy for me to return to the United States and to experience once more your warm hospitality.

As you know, I have been in Mexico, to celebrate the conclusion of the *Special Assembly for America of the Synod of Bishops.* The purpose of that important Meeting was to prepare the Church to enter the new Millennium and to encourage a new sense of solidarity among the peoples of the continent. Now I am happy to be able to bring this message to Mid America, on the banks of the Mississippi, in this historic city of St. Louis, the Gateway to the West.

I am grateful to you, Mr. President, for your courtesy in meeting me on my arrival. I likewise greet the Governor and authorities of the State of Missouri, as well as the Mayor of St. Louis and the other officials of the City and surrounding areas. So many people have offered their generous cooperation in preparation for this visit, and I am grateful to them all.

2. As Pastor of the universal Church, I am particularly happy to greet *the Catholic community of the Archdiocese of St. Louis,* with its rich spiritual heritage and its dynamic traditions of service to those in need. I wish to say a special word of appreciation to Archbishop Justin Rigali, who has been close to me since I became Pope twenty years ago. I am looking forward to being with the *priests, deacons, religious and laity* of this local Church, which has exercised such influence on the history of the Midwest.

With deep thanks I greet the Cardinals and Bishops. Their presence gives me an opportunity to send my *good wishes to the whole Province of St. Louis and its ecclesiastical Region, and to all the Dioceses of this country.* Although St. Louis is the only place I am able to visit at this time, I feel close to all the Catholics of the United States.

I express my friendship and esteem for my *fellow Christians,* for the *Jewish community* in America, for our *Muslim brothers and sisters.* I express my cordial respect for *people of all religions and for every person of good will.*

3. As history is retold, the name of St. Louis will be forever linked to the first transatlantic flight, and to *the immense human endeavor and daring behind the name: the "Spirit of St. Louis."*

You are preparing for the *bicentennial of the* Louisiana Purchase *made in 1804* by President Thomas Jefferson. That anniversary presents a challenge of religious and civic renewal to the entire community. It will be the opportunity to reassert the *"Spirit of St. Louis"* and to reaffirm the genuine truths and values of the American experience.

There are times of trial, tests of national character, in the history of every country. America has not been immune to them. One such time of trial is closely connected with St. Louis. Here, the famous Dred Scott case was heard. And in that case the Supreme Court of the United States subsequently declared an entire class of human beings—people of African descent—outside the boundaries of the national community and the Constitution's protection.

After untold suffering and with enormous effort, that situation has, at least in part, been reversed.

America faces a similar time of trial today. Today, the conflict is between *a culture that affirms, cherishes, and celebrates the gift of life,* and a culture that seeks to declare entire groups of human beings—the unborn, the terminally ill, the handicapped, and others considered "unuseful"—to be outside the boundaries of legal protection. Because of the seriousness of the issues involved, and because of America's great impact on the world as a whole, the resolution of this new time of testing will have profound consequences for the century whose threshold we are about to cross. My fervent prayer is that through the grace of God at work in the lives of Americans of every race, ethnic group, economic condition and creed, *America will resist the culture of death and choose to stand steadfastly on the side of life. To choose life*—as I wrote in this year's *Message for the World Day of Peace*—involves *rejecting every form of violence:* the violence of poverty and hunger, which oppresses so many human beings; the violence of armed conflict, which does not resolve but only increases divisions and tensions; the violence of particularly abhorrent weapons such as anti-personnel mines; the violence of drug trafficking; the violence of racism; and the violence of mindless damage to the natural environment.

Only a higher moral vision can motivate the choice for life. And the values underlying that vision will greatly depend on whether the nation continues to *honor and revere the family as the basic unit of society:* the family—teacher of love, service, understanding and forgiveness; the family—open and generous to the needs of others; the family—the great wellspring of human happiness.

4. Mr. President, dear friends. I am pleased to have another opportunity to thank the American people for the countless works of human goodness and solidarity which, from the beginning, have been such a part of the history of your country. At the same time I know that you will hear my plea to *open wide your hearts to the ever increasing plight and urgent needs of our less fortunate brothers and sisters throughout the world.*

This too—the spirit of compassion, concern and generous sharing—must be part of the *"Spirit of St. Louis."* Even more, it must be the renewed spirit of this "one nation, under God, with liberty and justice for all." God bless you all! God bless America!

"Light of the World" Youth Gathering

Kiel Center

Homily (Part I)

Dear Young People of St. Louis,
Dear Young People of the United States,
Praised be Jesus Christ!

1. Your warm and enthusiastic welcome makes me very happy. It tells me that tonight *the Pope belongs to you.* I have just been in Mexico City, to celebrate the conclusion of the Synod of Bishops for America. There I had the joy of being with many thousands of young people. And now, my joy continues here with you, so, yesterday the young people of Mexico, today *the young people of St. Louis and Missouri, and of the whole United States.*

2. We are gathered here this evening to listen to Jesus as he speaks to us through his word and in the power of the Holy Spirit.

We have just heard the Apostle Paul say to Timothy, his young fellow evangelizer: "Train yourself for devotion" (1 Tim 4:7). These are important words for every Christian, for everyone who truly seeks to follow the Lord and to put his words into practice. They are especially important for you, the young people of the Church. And so you need to ask yourselves: *what training am I doing in order to live a truly Christian life?*

You all know what "training" is, and what it signifies. In fact, we are here in the Kiel Center where many people train long and hard in order to compete in different sports. Today, this impressive stadium has become another kind of training ground—not for hockey or soccer or baseball or basketball—I'll say here nothing about football!—but for that training that will help you to live your faith in Jesus more decisively. This is the "training in devotion" that Saint Paul is referring to—the training that makes it possible for you *to give yourselves without reservation to the Lord and to the work that he calls you to do!*

3. I am told that there was much excitement in St. Louis during the recent baseball season, when two great players (Mark McGwire and Sammy Sosa) were competing to break the home-run record. You can feel the same great enthusiasm as you train for a different goal: *the goal of following Christ, the goal of bringing his message to the world.*

Each one of you belongs to Christ, and Christ belongs to you. At Baptism you were claimed for Christ with the Sign of the Cross; you received the Catholic faith as a treasure to be shared with others. In Confirmation, you were sealed with the gifts of the Holy Spirit and strengthened for your Christian mission and vocation. In the Eucharist, you receive the food that nourishes you for the spiritual challenges of each day.

I am especially pleased that so many of you had the opportunity today to receive *the Sacrament of Penance, the Sacrament of Reconciliation.* In this Sacrament you experience the

Savior's tender mercy and love in a most personal way, when you are freed from sin and from its ugly companion which is shame. Your burdens are lifted and you experience the joy of new life in Christ.

Your belonging to the Church can find no greater expression or support than by *sharing in the Eucharist every Sunday in your parishes.* Christ gives us the gift of his body and blood to make us one body, one spirit in him, to bring us more deeply into communion with him and with all the members of his Body, the Church. *Make the Sunday celebration in your parishes a real encounter with Jesus in the community of his followers:* this is an essential part of your "training in devotion" to the Lord!

4. Dear young friends, in the Reading we have just heard, the Apostle Paul tells Timothy: "Let no one have contempt for your youth" (1 Tim 4:12). He says this because *youth is a marvelous gift of God.* It is a time of special energies, special opportunities and special responsibilities. Christ and the Church need your special talents. Use well the gifts the Lord has given you!

This is the time of your "training", of your physical, intellectual, emotional and spiritual development. But this does not mean that you can put off until later your meeting with Christ and your sharing in the Church's mission. Even though you are young, *the time for action is now!* Jesus does not have "contempt for your youth." He does not set you aside for a later time when you will be older and your training will be complete. Your training will never be finished. Christians are always in training. You are ready for what Christ wants of you now. He wants you—all of you— *to be light to the world, as only young people can be light. It is time to let your light shine!*

In all my travels I tell the world about your youthful energies, your gifts and your readiness to love and serve. And wherever I go *I challenge young people*—as a friend—*to live in the light and truth of Jesus Christ.* I urge you to let his word enter your hearts, and then from the bottom of your hearts to tell him: *"Here I am Lord, I come to do your will!"* (cf. Heb 10:7).

**"Light of the World"
Youth Gathering**

Homily (Part II)

"You are the light of the world…Your light must shine before all."   Mt 5:14.16

Dear Young People,

1. Ask yourselves: Do I believe these words of Jesus in the Gospel? Jesus is calling you *the light of the world.* He is asking you *to let your light shine before others.* I know that in your hearts you want to say: "Here I am, Lord. Here I am. I come to do your will" (*Responsorial Psalm;* cf. Heb 10:7). *But only if you are one with Jesus can you share his light and be a light to the world.*

Are you ready for this?

Sadly, too many people today are living apart from the light—in a world of illusions, a world of fleeting shadows and promises unfulfilled. If you *look to Jesus,* if you *live the Truth that is Jesus,* you will have in you the light that reveals *the truths and values* on which to build your own happiness, while building a world of justice, peace and solidarity. Remember what Jesus said: "I am the light of the world; those who follow me will not walk in darkness, but will have the light of life" (cf. Jn 8:12).

Because Jesus is the Light, *we too become light* when we proclaim him. This is the heart of the Christian mission to which each of you has been called through Baptism and Confirmation. *You are called to make the light of Christ shine brightly in the world.*

2. When you were little, were you sometimes afraid of the dark? Today you are no longer children afraid of the dark. You are teenagers and young adults. But already you realize that there is another kind of darkness in the world: the darkness of doubt and uncertainty. You may feel the darkness of loneliness and isolation. Your anxieties may come from questions about your future, or regrets about past choices.

Sometimes the world itself seems filled with darkness. The darkness of children who go hungry and even die. The darkness of homeless people who lack work and proper medical care. The darkness of violence: violence against the unborn child, violence in families, the violence of gangs, the violence of sexual abuse, the violence of drugs that destroy the body, mind and heart. There is something terribly wrong when so many young people are overcome by hopelessness to the point of taking their own lives. And already in parts of this nation, laws have been passed which allow doctors to end the lives of the very people they are sworn to help. *God's gift of life is being rejected.* Death is chosen over life, and this brings with it the darkness of despair.

3. But you believe in the light (cf. Jn 12:36)! Do not listen to those who encourage you to lie, to shirk responsibility, to put yourselves first. Do not listen to those who tell you that chastity is *passé.* In your hearts you know that true love is a gift from God and respects his plan for the union of man and woman in marriage. Do not be taken in by *false values and deceptive slogans,* especially about your freedom. True freedom is a wonderful gift from God, and it has been a cherished part of your country's history. But when freedom is separated from truth, individuals lose their moral direction and the very fabric of society begins to unravel.

Freedom is not the ability to do anything we want, whenever we want. Rather, *freedom is the ability to live responsibly the truth of our relationship with God and with one another.* Remember what Jesus said: "you will know the truth and the truth will set you free" (Jn 8:32). Let no one mislead you or prevent you from seeing what really matters. Turn to Jesus, listen to him, and discover the true meaning and direction of your lives.

4. You are children of the light (cf. Jn 12:36)! *You belong to Christ,* and he has called you by name. Your first responsibility is to get to know as much as you can about him, in your parishes, in religious instruction in your high schools and colleges, in your youth groups and Newman Centers.

But you will get to know him truly and personally only through prayer. What is needed is that you talk to him, and listen to him.

Today we are living in an age of instant communications. But do you realize *what a unique form of communication prayer is?* Prayer enables us to meet God at the most profound level of our being. It connects us directly to God, the living God: Father, Son and Holy Spirit, in a constant exchange of love.

Through prayer you will learn to become the light of the world, *because in prayer you become one with the source of our true light, Jesus himself.*

5. Each of you has a special mission in life, and you are each called to be a disciple of Christ. Many of you will serve God in the vocation of Christian married life; some of you will serve him as dedicated single persons; some as priests and religious. But *all of you must be the light of the world.* To those of you who think that Christ may be inviting you to follow him in the priesthood or the consecrated life I make this personal appeal: I ask you to open your hearts generously to him; do not delay your response. The Lord will help you to know his will; he will help you to follow your vocation courageously.

6. Young friends, in the days and weeks and years ahead, for as long as you remember this evening, remember that the Pope came to the United States, to the City of St. Louis, to call *the young people of America* to Christ, to invite you to follow him. *He*

"Light of the World" Youth Gathering

came to challenge you to be the light of the world! "The light shines in the darkness and the darkness does not overcome it" (Jn 1:5). Jesus who has conquered sin and death reminds you: "I am with you always" (Mt 28:20). He says: "Courage! It is I; have no fear" (Mk 6:50).

On the horizon of this city stands the Gateway Arch, which often catches the sunlight in its different colors and hues. In a similar way, in a thousand different ways, you must *reflect the light of Christ through your lives of prayer and joyful service of others.* With the help of Mary, the Mother of Jesus, the young people of America will do this magnificently!

Remember: *Christ is calling you; the Church needs you; the Pope believes in you and he expects great things of you!*

Praised be Jesus Christ!

So I am prepared to return once more to play hockey! But if I will be able to, that is the question. Perhaps after this meeting, I will be a bit more ready!

Message to the Children

To the Children at Cardinal Glennon Children's Hospital

I am happy, dear children, during my visit to St. Louis, to be able to see some of you personally at the Kiel Center, and to be able to embrace you one by one.

You are all dear to my heart, even if I have not been able to see all of you today. I want the young boys and girls being taken care of at Cardinal Glennon Children's Hospital and all sick children everywhere to know that the Pope prays for each one of you.

You know how much Jesus loved children and how pleased he was to be with them. You too are very special to him. Some of you and your friends have suffered a lot and you feel the burden of what has happened to you. I want to encourage you to be patient and to stay close to Jesus, who suffered and died on the Cross out of love for you and me.

Surrounding you are other people who love you very much. Among them are the Franciscan Sisters of Mary; for many years they have faithfully administered this hospital. There are also those who actually take care of you and those who work hard to support the Cardinal Glennon Children's Hospital. And of course there are your families and friends who love you very much and want you to be strong and brave. I am happy to bless all of them.

Today I am thinking also about so many other sick people in the Archdiocese of St. Louis and beyond. I send my greetings to all the sick and suffering, and to the elderly, and I assure them of a special place in my daily prayers. They have a particularly fruitful role in the spiritual heart of the Church.

I invite all the sick to trust in Jesus who said: "I am the resurrection and the life" (Jn 11:25). In union with him, even our trials and sufferings are precious for the redemption of the world. May his Mother Mary accompany you and fill your hearts with joy. With my Apostolic Blessing.

From St. Louis, January 26, 1999

Joannes Paulus pp. II

Solemn Eucharistic Celebration

Homily

"In this way the love of God was revealed to us: God sent his only Son into the world so that we might have life through him."   1 Jn 4:9

Dear Brothers and Sisters,

1. In the Incarnation, God fully reveals himself in the Son who came into the world (cf. *Tertio Millennio Adveniente*, 9). Our faith is not simply the result of our searching for God. In Jesus Christ, it is God who comes in person to speak to us and to show us the way to himself.

The Incarnation also reveals the truth about man. In Jesus Christ, the Father has spoken the definitive word about our true destiny and the meaning of human history (cf. ibid., 5). *"In this is love: not that we have loved God, but that he loved us and sent his Son as an expiation for our sins"* (1 Jn 4:10). The Apostle is speaking of the love that inspired the Son to become man and to dwell among us. Through Jesus Christ we know how much the Father loves us. In Jesus Christ, by the gift of the Holy Spirit, each one of us can share in the love that is the life of the Blessed Trinity.

Saint John goes on: *"Whoever acknowledges that Jesus is the Son of God, God remains in him and he in God"* (1 Jn 4:15). Through faith in the Son of God made man we abide in the very heart of God: *"God is love, and whoever remains in love remains in God and God in him"* (1 Jn 4:16). These words open to us the mystery of the Sacred Heart of Jesus: the love and compassion of Jesus is the door through which the eternal love of the Father is poured out on the world. In celebrating this Mass of the Sacred Heart, *let us open wide our own hearts to God's saving mercy!*

2. In the Gospel reading which we have just heard, Saint Luke uses *the figure of the Good Shepherd* to speak of this divine love. The Good Shepherd is an image dear to Jesus in the Gospels. Answering the Pharisees who complained that he welcomed sinners by eating with them, the Lord asks them a question: Which of you, having a hundred sheep and losing one of them, would not leave the ninety-nine in the desert and go after the lost one until he finds it? "And when he does find it, he sets it on his shoulders with great joy and, upon his arrival home, he calls together his friends and neighbors and says to them: *'Rejoice with me because I have found my lost sheep'*" (Lk 15:5-6).

This parable highlights the joy of Christ and of our heavenly Father at every sinner who repents. God's love is a love that searches us out. *It is a love that saves.* This is the love that we find in the Heart of Jesus.

3. Once we know the love that is in the Heart of Christ, we know that every individual, every family, every people on the face of the earth can place their trust in that Heart. We have heard Moses say: *"You are a people sacred to the Lord, your God…the Lord set his heart on you and chose you…because the Lord loved you"* (Deut 7:6-8). From Old Testament times, the core of salvation history is *God's unfailing love and election, and our human answer to that love.* Our faith is our response to God's love and election.

Three hundred years have passed since December 8, 1698, when the Holy Sacrifice of the Mass was offered for the first time in what is now the City of St. Louis. It was the Feast of the Immaculate Conception of our Blessed Mother, and Father Montigny, Father Davion and Father St. Cosme set up a stone altar on the banks of the Mississippi River and offered Mass. These three centuries have been a *history of God's love poured out in this part of the United States,* and a history of generous response to that love.

In this Archdiocese, the commandment of love has called forth an endless series of activities for which—today—we give thanks to our heavenly Father. St. Louis has been the Gateway to the West, but it has also been the gateway of great Christian witness and evangelical service. In fidelity to Christ's command to evangelize, the first pastor of this local Church, Bishop Joseph Rosati—who came from the town of Sora, very near Rome—*promoted outstanding missionary activity from the beginning.* In fact, today we can count forty-six different Dioceses in the area which Bishop Rosati served. With great affection I greet your present Pastor, dear Archbishop Rigali, my precious collaborator in Rome. In the love of the Lord I greet the entire Church in this region.

In this area, numerous *Religious Congregations* of men and women have labored for the Gospel with exemplary dedication, generation after generation. Here can be found the American roots of the evangelizing efforts of the Legion of Mary and other associations of the *lay apostolate.* The work of the *Society for the Propagation of the Faith,* made possible by the generous support of the people of this Archdiocese, is a real sharing in the Church's response to Christ's command to evangelize. From St. Louis, Cardinal Ritter sent the first *Fidei Donum* priests to Latin America in 1956, giving practical expression to the exchange of gifts which should always be a part of the communion between the Churches. This solidarity within the Church was the central theme of last year's *Special Assembly for America of the Synod of Bishops,* and it is the central idea of the Apostolic Exhortation Ecclesia in America—the Church in America—which I have just signed and issued at the Shrine of Our Lady of Guadalupe in Mexico City.

4. Here, by the grace of God, *charitable activities* of every kind have been a vibrant part of Catholic life. *The Saint Vincent de Paul Society* has had a privileged place in the Archdiocese from the beginning. Catholic Charities have for years performed exceptional work in the name of Jesus Christ. Outstanding *Catholic health care services* have shown the human face of the loving and compassionate Christ.

Solemn Eucharistic Celebration

Catholic schools have proven to be of priceless value to generations of children, teaching them to know, love and serve God, and preparing them to take their place with responsibility in the community. Parents, teachers, pastors, administrators and entire parishes have sacrificed enormously to maintain *the essential character of Catholic education* as an authentic ministry of the Church and an evangelical service to the young. The goals of the *Strategic Pastoral Plan of the Archdiocese*—evangelization, conversion, stewardship, Catholic education, service to those in need—have a long tradition here.

Today, American Catholics are seriously challenged to *know and cherish this immense heritage of holiness and service.* Out of that heritage you must draw inspiration and strength for the *new evangelization* so urgently needed at the approach of the Third Christian Millennium. In the holiness and service of St. Louis's own Saint Philippine Duchesne, and of countless faithful priests, religious and laity since the Church's earliest days in this area, Catholic life has appeared in all its rich and varied splendor. *Nothing less is asked of you today.*

5. As the new evangelization unfolds, it must include a special emphasis *on the family and the renewal of Christian marriage.* In their primary mission of communicating love to each other, of being co-creators with God of human life, and of transmitting the love of God to their children, parents must know that they are fully supported by the Church and by society. The new evangelization must bring a fuller appreciation of *the family as the primary and most vital foundation of society,* the first school of social virtue and solidarity (cf. Familiaris Consortio, 42). *As the family goes, so goes the nation!*

The new evangelization must also bring out the truth that "the Gospel of God's love for man, *the Gospel of the dignity of the person and the Gospel of life are a single and indivisible Gospel"* (*Evangelium Vitae,* 2). As believers, how can we fail to see that abortion, euthanasia and assisted suicide are a terrible rejection of God's gift of life and love? And as believers, how can we fail to feel the duty to surround the sick and those in distress with the warmth of our affection and the support that will help them always to embrace life?

The new evangelization calls for *followers of Christ who are unconditionally pro-life:* who will proclaim, celebrate and serve the Gospel of life in every situation. A sign of hope is the *increasing recognition that the dignity of human life must never be taken away,* even in the case of someone who has done great evil. Modern society has the means of protecting itself, without definitively denying criminals the chance to reform (cf. *Evangelium Vitae,* 27). I renew the appeal I made most recently at Christmas for a consensus to end the death penalty, which is both cruel and unnecessary.

As the new millennium approaches, there remains another great challenge facing this community of St. Louis, east and west of the Mississippi, and not St. Louis alone, but the whole country: to *put an end to every form of racism,* a plague which your Bishops have called one of the most persistent and destructive evils of the nation.

6. Dear Brothers and Sisters, the Gospel of God's love, which we are celebrating today, finds its highest expression in the Eucharist. In the Mass and in Eucharistic Adoration we meet the merciful love of God that passes through the Heart of Jesus Christ. In the name of Jesus, the Good Shepherd I wish to make an appeal—an appeal to Catholics throughout the United States and wherever my voice or words may reach—especially to those who for one reason or another are separated from the practice of their faith. *On the eve of the Great Jubilee of the two thousandth anniversary of the Incarnation, Christ is seeking you out and inviting you back to the community of faith.* Is this not the moment for you to experience the joy of returning to the Father's house? In some cases there may still be obstacles to Eucharistic participation; in some cases there may be memories to be healed; *in all cases there is the assurance of God's love and mercy.*

The Great Jubilee of the Year 2000 will begin with the opening of the Holy Door in Saint Peter's Basilica in Rome: this is a powerful symbol of the Church—*open to everyone who feels a need for the love and mercy of the Heart of Christ.* In the Gospel Jesus says: *"I am the door; whoever enters through me will be saved, and will come in and go out and find pasture"* (cf. Jn 10:9).

Our Christian life can be seen as a great *pilgrimage to the house of the Father,* which passes through the door that is Jesus Christ. The key to that door is repentance and conversion. The strength to pass through that door comes from our faith and hope and love. For many Catholics, an important part of the journey must be to rediscover the joy of belonging to the Church, *to cherish the Church* as the Lord has given her to us, *as Mother and Teacher.*

Living in the Holy Spirit, the Church looks forward to the Millennium as a time of far-reaching spiritual renewal. The Spirit will truly bring about *a new springtime of faith* if Christian hearts are filled with new attitudes of humility, generosity and openness to his purifying grace. In parishes and communities across this land holiness and Christian service will flourish if *"you come to know and believe in the love God has for you"* (cf. 1 Jn 4:16).

Mary, Mother of Mercy, teach the people of St. Louis and of the United States to say yes to your Son, our Lord Jesus Christ!

Mother of the Church, on the way to the Great Jubilee of the Third Millennium, be the Star which safely guides our steps to the Lord!

Virgin of Nazareth, two thousand years ago you brought into the world the Incarnate Word: lead the men and women of the new Millennium to the One who is the true light of the world! Amen.

Solemn Eucharistic Celebration

Words at the end of Mass

Peace—the peace of Christ—to all: to my Brother Cardinals and Bishops—so many here today—the Pastors of the Church in America.

A special greeting to the Priests, who carry forward with love the daily pastoral care of God's people.

My thanks to you all for this beautiful liturgy!

I appreciate very much your enthusiastic participation and your spirit of prayer.

Again, I express my gratitude to Archbishop Rigali, your Pastor, and to everyone who cooperated in preparing this great event.

(Polish) I cordially greet my fellow Poles in America, particularly those living in St. Louis. I thank you for remembering me in your prayers. God bless you all!

A special word of affection goes to the sick, those in prison, and all who suffer in mind and body.

My gratitude and esteem go also to our brothers and sisters who, in a spirit of ecumenical friendship, have shared this wonderful moment with us.

Homily

"May the peoples praise you, O God; may all the peoples praise you."　　　Psalm 67:4

Dear Brothers and Sisters,

1. We are here together in this striking Cathedral Basilica to worship God and to let our prayer rise up to him like incense. In singing God's praises, *we remember and acknowledge God's dominion over creation and over our lives.* Our prayer this evening reminds us that our true mother-tongue is the praise of God, the language of Heaven, our true home.

We are gathered on what is already *the eve of a new Millennium*—by any standard a decisive turning-point for the world. As we look at the century we are leaving behind, we see that human pride and the power of sin have made it difficult for many people to speak their mother-tongue. In order to be able to sing God's praises we must relearn the language of humility and trust, the language of moral integrity and of sincere commitment to all that is truly good in the sight of the Lord.

2. We have just heard a moving Reading in which the Prophet Isaiah envisions a people returning from exile, overwhelmed and discouraged. We too sometimes experience the parched desert-land: our hands feeble, our knees weak, our hearts frightened. How often the praise of God dies on our lips and a song of lament comes instead! The Prophet's message is *a call for trust,* a call to courage, a call to hope for salvation from the Lord. How compelling, for all of us today, his exhortation: *"Be strong, fear not! Here is your God…he comes to save you"* (Is 35:3-4)!

3. Our gracious host, Archbishop Rigali, has invited to this Evening Prayer representatives of many different religious groups and sectors of civil society. I greet the Vice President of the United States of America, and the other civil authorities and community leaders present. I greet my brothers and sisters in the Catholic faith: *the members of the laity* who want to live their baptismal dignity ever more intensely in their efforts to bring the Gospel to bear on the realities of everyday life in society.

With affection *I greet my brother priests,* representing all the many zealous and generous priests of St. Louis and other Dioceses. My hope is that you will rejoice each day in your encounter—in prayer and in the Eucharist—with the living Jesus Christ, whose priesthood you share. I happily greet the *deacons of the Church* and encourage you in your liturgical, pastoral and charitable ministry. A special word of thanks goes to your wives and families for their supportive role in this ministry.

The many *Religious* who are here this evening represent thousands and thousands of women and men who have labored in the Archdiocese from the beginning. You are those who follow Christ by imitating his total self-giving to the Father and to the cause of his Kingdom. My appreciation and thanks go to each one of you.

I gladly address a special word of encouragement to the *seminarians.* You will be the priests of the new Millennium, working with Christ in the new evangelization; helping the Church, under the action of the Holy Spirit, to meet the demands of the new century. I pray each day that the Lord will make you "shepherds after his own heart" (Jer 3:15).

4. I am particularly pleased that *distinguished members of other Churches and Ecclesial Communities* have joined the Catholic community of St. Louis in this Evening Prayer. With hope and confidence let us continue to work together to realize the Lord's desire: "That they may all be one…that the world may believe" (Jn 17:21). My friendship and esteem go also to those of *all other religious traditions.* In particular I recall my long association with members of the Jewish faith, and my meetings in many parts of the world with my Muslim brothers and sisters. Today, divine Providence has brought us all together and enabled us to pray: *"O God, let all the nations praise you!"* May this prayer signify our shared commitment to ever greater understanding and cooperation.

5. I wish also to say a word of appreciation to the civic community of the entire metropolitan area, to all those associated with the City of St. Louis and committed to its human, cultural and social well-being. Your determination to meet the many urban challenges facing the community will help bring about a renewed *"Spirit of St. Louis"* to serve the cause of the city, which is the cause of its people and their needs. Of particular concern must be the training of young people for positive participation in the community. In this regard I share the Archdiocese's hope that *Cardinal Ritter College Prep,* sustained by the concerted support of all sectors, will be able to continue to give numerous young people the opportunity for quality education and genuine human advancement.

In the Church's name I express gratitude to everyone, including the business community, for their continuing support of many worthy charitable, social and educational services promoted by the Church.

6. *"O God, let all the nations praise you!"* (Ps 67)
At the end of this century—at once marked by unprecedented progress and by a tragic toll of human suffering—*radical changes in world politics leave America with a heightened responsibility* to be for the world an example of a genuinely free, democratic, just and humane society. There is a lesson for every powerful nation in the Canticle from the Book of Revelation which we have recited. It actually refers

to *the song of freedom* which Moses sang after he had led the people through the Red Sea, saving them from the wrath of the Pharaoh. The whole of salvation history has to be read in the perspective of that Exodus: *God reveals himself in his actions to defend the humble of the earth and free the oppressed.*

In the same way, in her *Magnificat* Canticle, Mary, the Mother of the Redeemer, gives us the key to understanding God's intervention in human history when she says: the Lord "has scattered the proud in the conceit of their hearts…and *exalted the lowly*" (Lk 1:51-52). From salvation history we learn that *power is responsibility:* it is service, not privilege. Its exercise is morally justifiable when it is used for the good of all, when it is sensitive to the needs of the poor and defenseless.

There is another lesson here: God has given us a moral law to guide us and protect us from falling back into the slavery of sin and falsehood. We are not alone with our responsibility for the great gift of freedom. The Ten Commandments are the charter of true freedom, for individuals as well as for society as a whole.

America first proclaimed its independence on the basis of self-evident moral truths. America will remain a beacon of freedom for the world as long as it stands by those moral truths which are the very heart of its historical experience. And so America: If you want peace, *work for justice.* If you want justice, *defend life.* If you want life, *embrace the truth*—the truth revealed by God.

In this way the praise of God, the language of Heaven, will be ever on this people's lips: "The Lord is God, the mighty…*Come then, let us bow down and worship.*" Amen.

Evening Prayer Service

Final Words

As my visit to St. Louis comes to an end, I wish to express my appreciation to *Vice President and Mrs. Gore* for greeting me before my departure for Rome. I thank those associated with the Federal Government for all that they have done to make this visit possible.

My gratitude goes to the Governor of the *State of Missouri,* and to the Mayor of the *City of St. Louis,* and to all the members of their staffs. I thank the Police and all those who have done so much for security and public order. I thank the civic and business communities of St. Louis for the support they have given.

The welcome extended to me by my *fellow Christians and by the members of other religious communities* has been most gracious. I hope you will accept my sincere thanks and the assurance of my friendship in the cause of ecumenism and interreligious dialogue and cooperation.

It has been a moving experience to visit the people of St. Louis. I would have wished to meet personally each one of the young people at the Kiel Center, and all the many other people at the Trans World Dome, and here in the Cathedral Basilica, as well as along the routes and at the Airport.

A word of thanks goes to *the Cardinals and my brother Bishops of the United States* who have come to St. Louis. It was a pleasure to know that so many other Dioceses sent representatives. I am grateful to you all.

In particular I wish to say thanks to *the local Church of St. Louis.* I am indebted to all the many dedicated people—organizers, committee members and volunteers—who have labored long and hard behind the scenes. Nor do I forget the hidden but effective support of all who prayed for the spiritual outcome of this event, especially *the contemplatives* in their monasteries. A special word of thanks and appreciation is due to *Archbishop Rigali,* who just two days ago celebrated his fifth anniversary as your dedicated Pastor.

A few months ago, a pilgrimage from St. Louis came to Rome. We met on the steps of St. Peters, where they sang to me: "Meet me in St. Louis…meet me at the Dome!" With God's help, we have done it. I will always remember St. Louis. I will remember all of you.

God bless St. Louis!

God bless America!

Epilogue

Let everyone join in the prayer of the Successor of Peter, invoking Christ who is "the way of conversion, communion and solidarity in America":

We thank you, Lord Jesus,
because the Gospel of the Father's love,
with which you came to save the world,
has been proclaimed far and wide in America
as a gift of the Holy Spirit
that fills us with gladness.
We thank you for the gift of your Life,
which you have given us by loving us to the end:
your Life makes us children of God,
brothers and sisters to each other.
Increase, O Lord, our faith and our love for you,
present in all the tabernacles of the continent.
Grant us to be faithful witnesses
to your Resurrection
for the younger generation of Americans,
so that, in knowing you, they may follow you
and find in you their peace and joy.
Only then will they know that they
are brothers and sisters
of all God's children scattered
throughout the world.
You who, in becoming man,
chose to belong to a human family,
teach families the virtues which filled with light
the family home of Nazareth.

May families always be united,
as you and the Father are one,
and may they be living witnesses
to love, justice and solidarity;
make them schools of respect,
forgiveness and mutual help,
so that the world may believe;
help them to be the source of vocations
to the priesthood and the consecrated life,
and all the other forms
of firm Christian commitment.
Protect your Church and the Successor of Peter,
to whom you, Good Shepherd, have entrusted
the task of feeding your flock.
Grant that the Church in America may flourish
and grow richer in the fruits of holiness.
Teach us to love your Mother, Mary,
as you loved her.
Give us strength to proclaim
your word with courage
in the work of the new evangelization,
so that the world may know new hope.
Our Lady of Guadalupe, Mother of America,
pray for us!

Pope John Paul II
Ecclesia in America —The Church in America

Credits

Executive Publisher: Archbishop Justin Rigali
Project Directors: Monsignor Richard Stika, Monsignor Ted Wojcicki,
    Monsignor Dennis Delaney, Reverend Henry Breier, Ms. Jennifer Stanard

Creative Director and Photo Editor: Patrick Henning
Art Director and Designer: Susan Klein-Shelton
Editorial Contributors: Reverend Larry Brennan, Patrick Henning
Production Assistants: Lisa Patton Vorst, David Lewis, Laura Puricelli, Laurie Ott,
    Melissa Dunbar, Anne Henning, Amy Grzina, Jennifer Duncan

Photography
Brauer Company
Dreyfus and Associates Photography
David W. Preston
Scott Raffe Photography
Tim Umphrey Sports Photography
Nancy Wiechec, Catholic News Service

Printing
Scholin Brothers Printing

Binding
Nicholstone

Paper
Warren Lustro Gloss

Fonts
Adobe Caslon, Bernhard Modern, Bodoni, Helvetica Neue

Photo Credits

Anheuser-Busch: 3 (E)

Brauer Company: 35 (top), 43 (bottom), 69 (bottom), 91, 99 (bottom), 112 (top), 132 (top)

Catholic News Service: 4, 5 (right), 6

Catholic News Service — Nancy Wiechec: 13 (both), 14, 16-17, 20, 22 (left), 25 (left), 26 (left), 28, 30, 32, 35 (left and right), 40 (bottom), 41, 45 (left), 46-47, 48 (top), 56, 60, 75 (both), 86 (bottom), 89 (bottom), 94 (bottom), 105 (top), 107, 111 (both), 113, 114 (bottom), 124 (bottom)

Dreyfus and Associates Photography: table of contents, 11, 31 (left), 34, 48 (bottom), 50 (right), 52-53, 58 (top), 59, 62-63, 64 (right), 65, 66, 68, 69, 74, 76-77, 80 (bottom right), 82-83, 84-85, 88 (both), 94 (top), 114 (top), 117 (left), 124 (top), 125, 128, 133

Richard C. Finke: 10 (top)

Richard Krauze: 22 (right)

McCarty Photography: 2

John Wm Nagel Photography: second title page

David W. Preston: 8, 15, 18 (left), 21, 23, 25 (right), 26 (right), 27, 31 (right), 36-37, 38, 39 (left), 42-43, 44, 49, 54-55, 58 (bottom), 70-71, 73 (left), 78 (left), 79, 80 (top right), 86 (top), 87, 92 (right), 93, 95, 96-97, 98-99, 100, 103, 104, 105 (bottom), 108-109, 110, 115, 122 (right), 126-127, 132 (both)

Scott Raffe Photography: 9, 12, 15, 19, 24, 29, 39 (right), 42 (left), 45 (right), 50 (left), 51, 61, 64 (left), 73 (right), 80 (left), 89 (top), 92 (left), 106, 117 (right), 122 (left), 129 (top)

St. Louis Convention & Visitors Commission: 10 (bottom)

Stan the Man, Inc.: 3 (G)

Time, Inc.: 5 (left)

Tim Umphrey Sports Photography: 18 (right), 40 (top), 57 (both), 71, 72, 78 (right), 81, 90-91, 102, 112 (bottom), 116, 118-119, 120-121, 123, 129 (bottom), 130-131.

United States Senate: 3 (F)